Kate Bush

THE KICK INSIDE

In-depth

Laura Shenton

"Being able to express oneself is what it's all about really."
- Kate Bush, The Liverpool Echo, February 1978

Kate Bush
THE KICK INSIDE

In-depth

Laura Shenton

WP
WYMER
PUBLISHING
Bedford, England

First published in 2021 by Wymer Publishing
Bedford, England www.wymerpublishing.co.uk Tel: 01234 326691
Wymer Publishing is a trading name of Wymer (UK) Ltd

Print edition (fully illustrated): **ISBN: 978-1-912782-59-8**

Edited by Jerry Bloom.
Proofread by Lin White of Coinlea.

eBook formatting by Coinlea.

A catalogue record for this book is available from the British Library.

Typeset by Andy Bishop / 1016 Sarpsborg
Cover design by 1016 Sarpsborg.
Cover photo © Pictorial Press / Alamy Stock Photo

Contents

Preface

The *Kick Inside* is the album that started it all. For Kate Bush, and indeed many in her strong fanbase her 1978 debut was certainly attention grabbing; it propelled her to fame and got the ball rolling for a phenomenal career as a much-appreciated musician and admired female talent.

As author of this book, it is my aim to offer an insight into *The Kick Inside* in a way that discusses the music in detail in relation to what Kate Bush's creative process was. I want to offer something factual rather than something that is peppered with my own opinion and interpretation of the music. You won't see statements in the lexicon of "this section is in the key of A and it therefore means X" or "I think this lyric means Y." For of course, the beauty of music is often in the ambiguity; it would be futile to throw a lot of my own opinions out there because it won't add anything to the literature if I do that.

The purpose of this book is to look at Kate Bush's debut album in terms of what she created at the time and how she went about it, as well as the impact that the album made and what its legacy and relevance are today. The facts based on what an artist says about their own work are often more important than the opinion of a music fan offering an enthusiastic narrative. Therefore, throughout this book you're going to see lots of quotes from vintage articles. I think it's important to corroborate such material as there will probably come a time when it is harder to source.

Personally, I think that *The Kick Inside*, and indeed the second album, *Lionheart*, are both phenomenal masterpieces of artistic beauty and musical wonder. It's fair of me to state that here but equally, I promise to be objective in how I present the content in this book; it won't be an exercise in heroine worship.

In the interest of transparency, I have no affiliation with Kate Bush or with any of her associates. This book is based on extensive research and relevant commentary.

KATE BUSH
HER ALBUM
THE KICK INSIDE

EMC 3223 also available on cassette

Featuring "WUTHERING HEIGHTS"

9

Chapter One

Why The Kick Inside?

T he *Kick Inside* is the blueprint that set Kate Bush up for the rest of her career. Although her sound inevitably changed throughout the eighties in particular, her debut album is memorable and iconic. Released on EMI Records in February 1978, the album got to number three in the UK chart, and around the world it got into the top ten in many countries. It was considered in *The Stage* in December 1978; "Kate Bush pins down the vaguely manic appeal of an artist whose individuality has shot her to the top in a remarkably short time."

The Kick Inside features thirteen distinctive songs. In particular, it includes the single that started it all for Kate Bush, 'Wuthering Heights'. In 1980, in a TV interview with *Profiles In Rock*, she said of her sudden success, "It was an incredible surprise. You know, you think, 'Well I'd like it to get in the charts,' and it gets in the charts and you think, 'Great! It's in the charts!' And next week it's still in the charts and it's going up. And I mean the last thing I thought was, 'No, it will never do it, you know, top five, no!' Top five! And each time you think, 'My God, it's just not going to do it.' In fact the morning it got there someone I hadn't met for a couple of years rang me up and said, 'Congratulations!' and I didn't understand what he was talking about and he said, 'Oh, you're now number one,' and I just went, 'Wow!'."

Regarding the speed at which she rose to fame and success, Kate was quoted in *Wireless* in September 1983; "I don't think anyone could ever by ready for anything like that. I mean, you don't really expect things like that to happen, and as far as I'm concerned that's the only time that will ever happen. I think it was very strange, very wonderful though. It was incredibly unreal and I still find it hard to believe."

From an early age, Kate Bush had an open mind towards music that went beyond the obvious. She was quoted in *Musician* in 1985; "Well, I think the first pop thing I ever heard which I really liked was 'Little Red Rooster' (by The Rolling Stones). I heard it in a car coming back from the shops and I thought it was fascinating. It was the first song I'd ever heard where the singer was actually singing out of tune. I don't mean that derogatorily. What I mean, I suppose, is that the record sounded so unconventional, and I just hadn't experienced anyone singing like that before... It was really a fantastic sound — the fact that someone wasn't singing quite in tune and, because of that, was getting a very different emotion out of it. But I suppose, really, I first became aware of pop music around the late sixties. I was hearing that sort of music through my two brothers and thinking just how good it was. But for the fact that my brothers were playing those records, I probably wouldn't have heard them, as my friends in school wouldn't have been listening to things like that! I think that was the earliest pop music that I really felt was good."

There is so much beauty in Kate Bush's early music in terms of how, from her lyrics and melodies alone, she was able to create something that was almost otherworldly. She was quoted in the *Reading Evening Post* in April 1979; "I like my songs to make people shiver."

No subject seemed to be off the table and consequently, *The Kick Inside* is full of imagination and intrigue. It was considered in the *Liverpool Echo* in February 1978; "The Tempestuous love story of Cathy and Heathcliff from the book *Wuthering Heights* is the basis for a haunting song that in just three weeks has turned the world of pop topsy-turvy... (Kate Bush) has arrived in the middle of the music world with her unique voice and songwriting talent with the subtlety of a mortar bomb. 'Wuthering Heights' is a song that most people don't even understand, such is the intensity of feeling and high-pitched singing that Kate puts into it… Her way is through poignant but perceptive lyrics on her songs which already bear the mark of true talent. She describes her form of songwriting as "method songwriting" in which she adopts the pose of an inanimate object to approach a subject in a new way. On the song 'Kite', for example, she uses that remarkable voice to paint a lyrical picture of the dipping and soaring movement of a kite. Closing the album is its title track, 'The Kick Inside' which she wrote after hearing a traditional folk song about a deep love between a sister and a brother. After hearing the album and listening to her you can only conclude that there is a bright future ahead for Kate Bush. A future we can all share."

As an artist, Kate Bush was very unique in terms of how when it came to ideas for songs, she didn't go for the obvious choices. In an interview with MTV in 1985, she said, "I think everyone at some times feels misunderstood, but I can't think of any song that I would say was truly autobiographical. There's something of me in every song, in that I'm expressing something I'm hoping is interesting. But I don't think they're truly autobiographical comments in any way."

On the *The Kick Inside* promotional record Kate said; "I think maybe the reason I write songs is maybe I need to express myself. That I need to be heard by people, maybe just to feel that I am someone for some reason. But I don't really think it matters why as long as what I'm doing has some purpose."

Kate was quoted in *Trouser Press* in July 1978; "Every night for a couple of hours I'd sing and play. When I was fifteen my family thought it would be a good idea to maybe meet some people in the music business and see if I could get some response from my songs. I think they were pleased to see I had something I could release myself in. They neither encouraged me nor discouraged me, they just let me be myself, which is something I'll always thank them for… my brother had a friend who'd been in the record business for a couple of years. He came around to listen to me. I put twenty to thirty of my songs on a tape and he'd take it to record companies. Of course there was no response; you wouldn't be able to hear a thing, just this little girl with a piano going 'yaaaa yaaaa' for hours on end. The songs weren't that good. They were okay, but... I could sing in key but there was nothing there. It was awful noise; it was really something terrible. My tunes were more morbid and more negative. That was a lot of people's comment: they were too heavy. But then a lot of people are saying that about my current songs. The old ones were quite different musically, vocally, and lyrically."

Whilst Kate's commercial success came in the late seventies, she had been working hard with her music for a good while before that. In 1972, it was a family friend by the name of Ricky Hopper who presented Kate's earliest demo recordings to a record company. When no interest was shown, Hopper got in touch with an old friend, Dave Gilmour. Upon listening to Kate, Gilmour was impressed. Kate was quoted in *Record Mirror* in February 1978; "One day, along comes this friend of my brother's. He worked in the record business himself, and thought he might be able to help me make some contacts. Well, he knew Pink Floyd from Cambridge and he asked Dave Gilmour to hear me. I was absolutely terrified at the prospect of meeting him, but he was so sweet and kind, so human."

Kate's song that was eventually recorded for her 1990 album, *This Woman's Work*, 'Passing Through Air', was recorded at Dave Gilmour's home studio in 1973. The recordings were sent to various record companies but still to no avail.

Kate was quoted in *Trouser Press* in July 1978; "Dave (Gilmour) was doing his guardian angel bit and scouting for talent. He'd already found a band called Unicorn in a pub and was helping them. He came along to see me and he was great, such a human, kind person — and genuine. He said, 'It looks as if the only way you can do it is to put at most three songs on a tape and we'll get them properly arranged.' He put up the money for me to do that, which is amazing. No way could I have afforded to do anything like that. EMI heard it and I got the contract."

It was in 1975 that Dave Gilmour decided to step things up a level in his mission to get record companies interested in Kate's music. A short demo was professionally made in the June of that year at AIR Studios (Kate was quoted in *TV Week* in October 1978; "It must have cost (Gilmour) a fortune, but he didn't want anything out of it."). In the July, whilst Pink Floyd were working on *Wish You Were Here* at Abbey Road Studios, Gilmour played Kate Bush's demo tape to EMI's Bob Mercer. Mercer's immediate interest was such that by 1976, Kate Bush had secured a contract with EMI. She was given a small advance.

It was reported in *Superpop* in February 1979; "With £3,000 in the bank (courtesy of EMI) Kate spent the next two years under wraps, perfecting her pitch and piano technique, writing songs and generally preparing for her recording debut." Kate Bush certainly worked hard to get where she wanted to be. She was quoted in the same feature; "I remember I'd spend hours locked away in this little room with my piano, screeching my head off, in fact, I must have driven my family bonkers."

In getting her music career off the ground, and under the continued mentorship of Dave Gilmour, Kate was signed to EMI on the strength of her two songs, 'The Man With The Child In His Eyes' and 'Berlin' (which was later re-titled as 'The Saxophone Song'). Both such recordings were engineered by Geoff Emerick with Gilmour doing the executive production in 1975. However, most of the recordings for *The Kick Inside* took place in the summer of 1977 under the production of Andrew Powell.

Whilst developing her musical talents, Kate also studied dance and mime. She was quoted in *Tune In* in December 1978; "Once I got the contract I presumed things would happen. I didn't go on holiday in case they called me to do some recording. But nothing happened. Finally I decided to study dance because I felt at least that would be something progressive. There's an awful lot of dance training in mime and I found it very difficult because I'd never danced before. A lot of the other people in the classes were good and I was useless. I looked an idiot for months and I used to get so depressed and frustrated because I couldn't do it but challenge is very important to me and I was really tough with myself to carry on and stop looking a fool. If you don't dare a little you won't progress." In an interview with BBC Radio in 1979, she said; "I trained for a couple of years at a dance school... but it wasn't really mime, it was more modern dance. But I learned an awful lot from that, I really did."

Kate was quoted in *Wireless* in September 1983; "I wanted to do something that would show my name creatively, that it would hopefully complement the music, so I decided to take up dancing. I saw a performance by a mime artist called Lindsay Kemp and I thought that's really what I wanted to do, that kind of movement and combine it with music. So, I spent the next two years writing songs and just dancing. After about eighteen months, I went on to be a singer in a band. We started doing gigs around local pubs, doing other people's songs. After we had been doing that for just a couple of months, the record company decided it was time for me to do my own."

Regarding meeting Lindsay Kemp, Kate said in a TV appearance on *Multi-Coloured Swap Shop* in 1979, "I just went to see a show one night. And it was incredible! I couldn't believe what this guy was doing on the stage, in a night. He was completely demanding the audience's attention... I was just at tears at the end of the show. And I went to some of his lessons and he just opened up a new world for me, the fact that you can express so much with your body. And I thought, 'well you know maybe I can combine that with singing as well.' So I went along and started taking some proper lessons because it's important to discipline your body. And I did a couple years at a place in Covent Garden, like five days a week. And I really enjoyed it."

Of The Dance Centre in London's Covent Garden where she trained with Lindsay Kemp, Kate was quoted in *Record Mirror* in February 1978; "I loved that. It's the only place you can go and learn to dance without qualifications, which I didn't have. You pay by lesson, and even though I was sixteen and had never danced before, I did make great progress."

Overall, Kate's performing arts training wasn't particularly strict. That's not to say that she wasn't dedicated though. She was quoted in *Tune In* in December 1978; "I love the violin and I'd really like to try it again but I just didn't like being taught because I do feel very strongly that music should be free-form expression. I think frustration is the most important part of learning. You're forced to carry on until you can do it, at least I am. And when you get it out it feels so good. Teaching yourself the piano has its advantages, for instance, I can read chords, but I can't read notes. It's easy to give in but I was very determined to get it absolutely right."

Kate was quoted in the *New Zealand Listener* in December 1978; "Folk was my first introduction when I was just a baby. My brothers were into folk music, the traditional English and Irish — it couldn't help but have an influence on you when you're so young. In Ireland it's so strong, my mother's Irish and sometimes all day there would be fiddlers and everyone would dance in the garden. My brothers and myself owe a lot to her, she's got the musical gift and we're all into music."

Kate made good use of the time she had in between getting

signed and actually going into the studio to make *The Kick Inside*. In an interview with MTV in 1985, she said, "I had a recording contract, but I didn't know when I was going to be making the first album, and I had, in a way, time to kill and use until that point. And I had very little experience — certainly in the business, I mean coming straight from school. And I had almost two clear years of going to the dance school, learning to dance, getting more control over my body, and writing. Just using the time generally as a kind of foundation for what was to happen next when the album was released and the single was very successful. I think without having used the time like that, things could've been very different for me. I was very lucky."

On the *The Kick Inside* promotional record Kate said; "Hello everyone. This is Kate Bush and I'm here with my new album *The Kick Inside* and I hope you enjoy it. The album is something that has not just suddenly happened. It's been years of work because since I was a kid, I've always been writing songs and it was really just collecting together all the best songs that I had and putting them on the album, really years of preparation and inspiration that got it together. As a girl, really, I've always been into words as a form of communication. And even at school I was really into poetry and English and it just seemed to turn into music with the lyrics — that you can make poetry go with music so well, that it can actually become something more than just words — it can become something special."

'Wuthering Heights' was written not long before it was time to go into the studio to record *The Kick Inside* in July 1977. It was in March 1977 that the song was written during a full moon. In an interview with BBC Radio in 1979, upon being asked "Did you compose 'Wuthering Heights' after you joined EMI?" Kate explained; "Oh yeah. That was just before I made the first album."

Kate wrote in the first issue of the *Kate Bush Club* magazine in January 1979; "Well, I wrote 'Wuthering Heights' in my flat, sitting at the upright piano one night in March at about midnight. There was a full moon and the curtains were open, and every time I looked up for ideas, I looked at the moon. Actually, it came quite easily. I couldn't seem to get out of the chorus — it had a really circular feel to it, which is why it repeats. I had originally written something more complicated, but I couldn't link it up, so I kept the first bit and repeated it. I was really pleased, because it was the first song I had written for a while, as I'd been busy rehearsing with the KT Band. I felt a particular want to write it, and had wanted to write it for quite a while. I remember my brother John talking about the story, but I couldn't relate to it enough. So I borrowed the book and read a few pages, picking out a few lines. So I actually wrote the song before I had read the book right through. The name Cathy helped, and made it easier to project my own feelings of want for someone so much that you hate them. I could understand how Cathy felt. It's funny, but I heard a radio programme about a woman who was writing a book in Old English, and she found she was using words she didn't know, but when she looked them up she found they were correct. A similar thing happened with 'Wuthering Heights': I put lines in the song that I found in the book when I read it later. I've never been to Wuthering Heights, the place, though I would like to, and someone sent me a photo of where it's supposed to be."

Kate knew what she wanted. The original plan for the cover art of *The Kick Inside* had been decided by EMI. They wanted to use a photo of Kate in a pink dance leotard that had been taken by Gered Mankowitz. Kate's uncertainty about the decision was based on the fact that she wanted to be recognised for her music and not her body. The time it took for the promotional material to be finalised was such that it was already Christmas by then and EMI decided that it would be better to do a debut release in the new year. However, a demo of 'Wuthering Heights' had already been given to London's Capital Radio DJs, Eddie Pumer and Tony Myatt. Consequently, they gave the song an airing before the end of 1977. Prior to that, EMI had actually written to the radio stations asking them not to give the demo any airplay on the basis that an early reveal could compromise the anticipation and publicity they were trying to build. Pumer and Myatt though, either didn't get the message or chose to ignore it.

When 'Wuthering Heights' was released in January 1978, it was given generous airplay on radio. Although it wasn't reviewed positively by all of the music media, the uniqueness of the track was such that it was attention grabbing. Kate's vocals combined with the fact that lyric sheets weren't readily available along with the single's release ensured that whether or not people liked the song, most didn't have much of an idea of what it was about. Enter Capital Radio DJ, Jonathan King; when he sat in for Kenny Everett on his Saturday lunchtime show, he played 'Wuthering Heights' one line at a time, pausing it to read from a lyric sheet that had been given to him by EMI. An excellent idea but it still didn't quite clarify what 'Wuthering Heights', or indeed Kate Bush, was all about.

In the same month of its release, 'Wuthering Heights' was reviewed in *Melody Maker*; "Bizarre. Kate is a complete newcomer, is nineteen, was first unearthed by David Gilmour, and has spent time with mime coach to the stars Lindsay Kemp... the theatre influence comes through strongly on the cover... The orchestration is ornate and densely packed, but never overflows its banks, Kate's extraordinary vocals skating in and out, over and above. Reference points are tricky, but possibly a cross between Linda Lewis and Macbeth's three witches is closest. She turns the famous examination text by Emily Brontë into a glorious soap opera trauma."

So was Kate Bush a big fan of the book that she'd based her song on? Well, not necessarily. She was quoted in the *New*

Zealand Listener in December 1978; "*Wuthering Heights* is really the only book in that era I've read. They tend to be extremely over-romantic in that period, especially the women. I like a really extensive story with levels. I enjoy science fiction, especially Kurt Vonnegut. He's a mixture of humour and tragedy, I really like him." Kate stated in the *Kate Bush Club* magazine in 1984; "The only Brontë work I have ever read is *Wuthering Heights*."

On a TV appearance on *Multi-Coloured Swap Shop* in 1979, Kate explained what drew her attention to the Emily Brontë book; "Well it was originally from a TV series years ago and I'd just caught the very end of it. And it was like really freaky, because there's this hand coming through the window and whispering voices and I've always been into that sort of thing, you know, and it just hung around in my head. And the year before last I read the book and that was it, I had to write a song about it."

In 1980, in a TV interview with *Profiles In Rock*, Kate elaborated, "I just walked into the room and caught the end of this programme. And I am sure one of the reasons it stuck so heavily in my mind was because of the spirit of Cathy and as a child I was called Cathy, it later changed to Kate. It was just a matter of exaggerating all my bad areas, because she's a really vile person, she's just so headstrong and passionate and crazy, you know?"

Kate wrote in the first issue of the *Kate Bush Club* magazine in January 1979; "One thing that really pleases me is the amount of positive feedback I've had from the song, though I've heard that the Brontë Society think it's a disgrace. A lot of people have read the book because of the song and liked it, which I think is the best thing about it for me. I didn't know the book would be on the GCE syllabus in the year I had the hit, but lots of people have written to say how the song helped them. I'm really happy about that."

In an interview with BBC Radio in 1979, Kate said; "When I was at school, yeah (poetry) was my thing. And then I got into songs so I forgot about that then." However, her rapport with language and how to convey character through song was undeniable. She said in a TV interview on *Razzmatazz* in 1981, "When you're writing a song you've got to think of the character who's singing the song, who often isn't yourself. And that character will be in a particular situation, either an unhappy one, or in a certain room, with a certain person. And I think with all these things, you actually mentally push yourself into it, to write the song so that you'll be closest to that atmosphere."

On the promotional record released for *The Kick Inside*, Kate said; "This next song's called 'Wuthering Heights' and it's my single in England. It's from the novel called *Wuthering Heights* — you probably might know it better as the film. It's about the end of the film where Cathy has actually died and she's coming back as a spirit across the moors to come and get Heathcliff again. And it just struck me very strongly because it shows a lot about human beings and how if they can't get what they want, they will go to such extremes in order to do it. This is exactly what she did. She wouldn't even be alone when she was dead. She had to come back and get him. I just found it really amazing."

Perhaps Kate's fascination was centred more on the dynamics between the two main characters rather than the literature itself. She was quoted in *Pulse* in April 1984; "I really enjoyed the energy between those two." In an interview with MTV in 1985, Kate said, "The idea of a relationship that even when one of them is dead, they will not leave the other one alone, I found that fascinating… But a very nice story and the sense of how even when she's dead she has to come back for him. Possessive lady."

It seems that Kate was perhaps more captivated by the characters than the literature itself. Kate was quoted in *TV Week* in October 1978; "I developed a kind of fascination with Cathy after I saw the last ten minutes of the television series where she was at the window and cutting herself with the glass. It always stuck in my brain… It was probably a lot to do with the fact that her name was Cathy — and I was always called that as a child. My feeling about it was so strong that it kept coming back to me again and again. Then I read the book and discovered that Emily Brontë had her birthday on the same day as me, July 30th, and I really, really wanted to write a song about it all."

Kate eventually revealed that she didn't actually read the classic Emily Brontë book until much later on. In a TV interview on *Ask Aspel* in 1978, Kate said, "I hadn't read the book, that wasn't what inspired it. It was a television series they had years ago and I just managed to catch the very last few minutes, where there was a hand coming through the window, and blood everywhere, and glass. And I just didn't know what was going on and someone explained the story, and it was just hanging around for years. So I read the book, in order to get the research right, and wrote the song."

Years later, Kate clarified her position. She said in a TV interview with VH-1 in 1990; "I'm not actually a big Emily Brontë fan. A lot of people think I am, they presume I am. It just goes with this whole preconception they have of me as a sort of big Brontë fan, a Tolkien fan, the pre-Raphaelite lady. Which I think is actually a very big misconception. For me, 'Wuthering Heights' is the ultimate love story. You just cannot get beyond the passion that they cover there. You know, it's a love affair that goes beyond death — they will not be stopped by nature's boundaries."

Kate went to Germany and then to Holland in February 1978 to promote 'Wuthering Heights'. She made her first appearance on German TV on a rock music show called *Scene 78*. The show was filmed in a disused train station. Her debut appearance on Dutch TV was broadcast in the May. Against the backdrop of an amusement park by the name of De Efteling, 'Moving', 'Wuthering Heights', 'Them Heavy People', 'Strange Phenomena', 'The Man With The Child In His Eyes' and 'The Kick Inside' were performed.

In terms of its success as a single, 'Wuthering Heights' was a steady chart climber. It was at number forty-two on 7th February and then a week later it was at number twenty-seven. This was the point at which Kate Bush was starting to become a household name and was invited to perform on *Top Of The Pops* in mid February. The UK media were now keenly interested in the enchanting singer who also made TV appearances on *Saturday Night At The Mill* and *Magpie* in the same month. It was asserted in *The Stage* in March 1978; "On the strength of recent appearances on BBC One's *Top Of The Pops* and *Saturday Night At The Mill*, I rate Kate Bush as the most interesting girl singer to emerge for some time." By the end of the month, 'Wuthering Heights' was at number five in the UK singles chart. Come March 7th, the song was at number one. It had already gone silver and it wasn't long after this that it went gold. It stayed on the top spot for four weeks.

The success of 'Wuthering Heights' served as excellent promotion for *The Kick Inside*. The album came out in the February. Kate said of the song in a TV appearance on *Multi-Coloured Swap Shop* in 1979, "It means an awful lot. I mean, that's really why my name is known — because of that song, and because of the book."

It was reported in *Tune In* in December 1978; "Her extraordinary first single 'Wuthering Heights', which she wrote after watching the film on television, enabled Kate to move into the number one spot for such an astonishing length of time that she practically bought the freehold. She'd barely vacated the premises when her second single, 'The Man With The Child In His Eyes', a haunting look at adolescent fantasy which she wrote four years ago, plus an album of her own songs, *The Kick Inside*, won her a gold record, proving that Kate Bush, far from being a one-hit wonder, was definitely something."

It was in the first week of April that *The Kick Inside* peaked at number three. It was in the same week that 'Wuthering Heights' had its last week at number one. Many in the media were fascinated about what it was that made Kate Bush such an overnight success. Many theories were offered on the subject. It was asserted in *Superpop* in February 1979; "Kate went into the studio and commenced work on her debut album, *The Kick Inside*, which was released to several less than favourable reviews at the beginning of '78. The fact that the album still succeeded in making the top five was largely due to the huge success of her wavering 'Wuthering Heights' single — a high-pitched, haunting song based on the book of the same name (surprise, surprise) and which occupied the number one spot on the singles chart for several weeks on end. Kate was now catapulted firmly into the limelight. When her next single, 'The Man With The Child In His Eyes' also shot into the top five, Kate proved that without a doubt she possessed the Midas touch."

Despite how interested the media were in who Kate Bush was as a person in the late seventies, she was still seen by many as a bit of an enigma. It was considered in the *Newcastle Journal* in January 1979; "The word for Kate Bush is enigmatic. This year's top girl singer isn't putting all her cards on the table. She may give all her considerable intensity to her music, but she isn't revealing too much as a person. For a twenty-year-old who has suddenly been catapulted into the crazy world of pop stardom, she remains her private self — uncompromising, logical and disciplined in her work."

In February 1979, *Superpop* described Kate; "Despite her protestations, Bush is undeniably beautiful. Even if she doesn't enjoy being a female with a flawless face and figure, it's very obvious that her army of male followers do, as sackfuls (sic) of fan mail bear testament to. The fact that people actually bother to write to her never ceases to amaze Kate. In fact any compliment she ever receives about her work is invariably met with ecstatic, almost childlike, delight. We know that Kate is a vegetarian. That she loves cats, chocolate, David Bowie and Steely Dan. That she is very rich — to the point of giving cars as presents and tacking a studio onto her doctor daddy's house. But as a person she remains an enigma. The word most often used to describe her is invariably "nice" and many a frustrated journalist has tried (and failed) to penetrate her friendly, poised, polite exterior and expose a few personality pimples lurking beneath the flawless flesh. Seemingly she has none. She is kind, considerate and always good natured. She naturally admits to some faults but other people never get to see them. Whether you love her or loathe her (there's no in-between) the talented, individual that is Kate Bush is most undoubtedly for real. A certified, genuine person."

Kate was quoted in the *Newcastle Journal* in January 1979; "I think I know when to speak out and when to be tolerant. I used to wish I were a man, but now I'm happy to be a woman. I now believe that my looks don't get in the way of being accepted as a musician — I've surmounted that hurdle. I'll always be tough on myself, but I find the strength in being alone, fighting a battle and emerging satisfied that I've done my best. Perhaps that's what is strange about me. I grasp any chance of a family get-together, because I love my parents and brothers. But looking back, maybe the happiest times of all are when I've been alone, in an emotional state because a new song is beginning to flow."

It is difficult to classify Kate Bush's music into any particular genre. There are elements of rock and pop on *The Kick Inside* but it isn't without its moments, even when it comes to reggae. Yep, reggae! In the second issue of the *Kate Bush*

Club magazine in summer 1979, Kate wrote; "People haven't noticed that 'Kite' is a Bob Marley song." (of course, it's not *actually* a Bob Marley song. Kate's comment was made in the context of this: "'Wow' is a song about the music business — not just rock music but show business in general, including acting and theatre. People say that the music business is about rip-offs, the rat race, competition, strain, people trying to cut you down and so on, and though that's all there, there's also the magic. It was sparked off when I sat down to try and write a Pink Floyd song, something spacey; though I'm not surprised no one has picked that up, it's not really recognisable as that — in the same way that people haven't noticed that 'Kite' is a Bob Marley song, and 'Don't Push Your Foot On The Heartbrake' is a Patti Smith song.").

How about progressive rock? Art rock? Art pop? Avant garde? Could *The Kick Inside* be classified under any of those genres? Well, maybe. But really, what would be the value of trying to pigeonhole an album that is so unique? Does it have to be put in a category as a means of being able to better understand it? I would argue that it doesn't.

Technically, Kate's singing voice is so attention grabbing because it has so many elements to it; a high soprano that is also capable of some beautifully rounded lower notes outside of the range that her high notes would suggest. As such, the vocals that first drew the public's attention to Kate Bush are arguably beyond classification. It can't simply be said that she's a soprano or an alto. It goes beyond that. In a TV appearance on *Multi-Coloured Swap Shop* in 1979, upon being asked "You do have an amazing range, don't you; has it ever been sort of written down, how far you can go?", Kate answered, "Oh, no. That's the last thing I'd do, because if you set yourself a limit then you're probably never going to get over it."

It was considered in *Trouser Press* in July 1978; "Her voice! Depending on your reaction it's either Minnie Mouse or the heavenly host. Kate sings up there where Laura Nyro and Joni Mitchell have sometimes tried to reach, but with an important difference: she's not striving, that's where she's at home. And it's not an affectation, feminine or otherwise. The conviction with which she sails along at that stratospheric pitch makes the music seem eerie, driven, and finally tough, despite its aerial quality. It didn't take me long to conclude that Kate was one of those genuine originals that may not be destined for mass acceptance (most people I know dislike the record), but should be reckoned with on the basic of her creative uniqueness alone."

Kate Bush's vocals went beyond what any other pop singers were doing at the time. If the narrative of the lyrics or the journey of a melody demanded it, Bush would scream or belt accordingly. In an interview with BBC Radio in 1982, she was asked about how people first reacted to the unusual pitch of her vocals when 'Wuthering Heights' came out. She answered; "I think there were a lot of different reactions, some people really liked it, some people really didn't, and other people found it very amusing. For me, really, I just see it as a phase of my writing where I was just into playing around with that kind of range. And I find it changes, I mean as far as I'm concerned that's an old style for me now. But of course a lot of people still see that as being me now. But that's just part of the time situation where for a lot of people they will always think of me as 'Wuthering Heights' and nothing else."

While Kate's voice was often a major focus when it came to her rise to fame in the late seventies, it is important to consider that the structure of her songs are not so "out there" that they're not radio friendly; they are structured in a way that is accessible with verses and choruses. It is feasible to say that whilst they are distinctive, they don't break the rules of music theory to the extent that they require immense effort to listen to.

There are so many beautiful moods that feature on *The*

Kick Inside. Even though some of the themes of the songs are a bit unconventional, there are many relatable emotions expressed throughout: love, pain, inspiration, fear, intensity, uncertainty and so on. Essentially, *The Kick Inside* covers a lot of ground in one album. Themes of life and death are certainly not avoided. 'Wuthering Heights' is a candid expression of the character Catherine Earnshaw's torment as she yearns for Heathcliff. The album is also very exploratory in the range of locations it invites the listener to visit in their mind, from the windy moors to a Berlin bar. It is exciting to think that perhaps when Kate Bush made *The Kick Inside*, she was uninhibited in her ideas of the themes and feelings to explore through song; as someone who was just in her late teenage years, it is possible that the pressures of needing to be commercially viable in her art weren't at the front of her mind. We'll never know, but nevertheless, the candid and unapologetic use of imagery in *The Kick Inside* is certainly fascinating and enchanting.

Clearly, Kate wasn't outwardly angry, working class, or male — all aspects that contributed towards her standing out in the pop music scene of the late seventies. Her background was of notable difference; a doctor's daughter who had grown up in a musical household with supportive and encouraging family. In an interview with BBC Radio in 1979, Kate said, "I think by what you think and how you are, you attract things to you. I think if you are a negative unhappy person a lot of negative unhappy things could happen to you. I really believe in that, yeah."

On the *The Kick Inside* promotional record, Kate said; "I think life is all about your attitude and how you actually see things. I was lucky enough to be born into a family that consists of very observant people. They're very aware of people's motivations and why they do things. I think I'm very lucky because a lot of that has rubbed off on me. Since I've been a kid, I've always been aware of observing people and trying to observe myself and why I do things. It's such an incredibly fascinating process the way people work, I can't help but be inspired by all that goes around me. It's just incredible... I think I was very lucky because when I was a small child, my brothers were extremely musical. They were into traditional music: English and Irish folk. They were always playing stuff on the record players and had their own bands to go around the clubs. I got quite involved with it. I would sing along with them and sing harmonies. I think it was important because when you are very young, your mind is so open for new stimulus and direction. I think it was given to me then, so I didn't really have to spend maybe ten years finding out what I was here for. I think that's been an important part of my life."

It was reported in *Tune In* in December 1978; "Still only twenty, music has always been a part of her life. She began writing songs when she was eleven and grew up in a loving, caring family always ready with help, advice and encouragement. Her father, a doctor, plays well and one of her brothers, Paddy, makes and plays musical instruments and appears on Kate's albums. Her other brother, John, is a poet and writer and is married with two sons."

As was reported in *Superpop* in February 1979; "Kate Bush is, at twenty, already a star. Her short story may not be a classic case of rags to riches — but it does nevertheless, exude a strong fairytale flavour. The Bush background is impeccably middle class — her father is a GP, and it was in this safe, secure sanctuary that Kate's embryonic talents unfurled, flowered and eventually flourished. Before she was even eleven, the Bush baby had taught herself to play the family piano and it was around this time she first put pen to paper producing piles of poetry, prose and eventually, and inevitably, several songs. She left school at sixteen with ten O levels (including distinctions in English and music), and a brain bulging with musical ideas."

There is a sense that Bush was always very sure and very

determined in what she wanted to do with her life. Her reasons for leaving school were established. She was quoted in the same feature; "I knew I had to leave school then, I wanted to do something in music and I had to get away from the alternative career opportunities being rammed down my throat."

She said in a TV appearance on *Multi-Coloured Swap Shop* in 1979, "I think I've always wanted to record, since I was a kid, that's what I wanted to do, I wanted to be, if not a songwriter, a singer. And I'd never thought I'd be a singer, and I still in a way really don't consider myself a singer. And it's just fantastic for me that other people do. It's great."

She was quoted in *Wireless* in September 1983; "I had finished taking my O levels at school and was coming up to the stage where you start thinking about A levels at the University. And I wasn't really into the idea of going to University, so I thought I should leave school and concentrate on my career, already having signed a contract with the record company."

Financially, Kate was in an excellent position to get her career in music going from a young age. Added to that, who she knew was arguably an effective vehicle for her too. As was explained in *Superpop* in February 1979; "An inheritance from an aunt who had died gave Kate the financial security she needed to follow her own mind and so for a while she continued to create within the comfortable confines of her own family."

When 'Wuthering Heights' was soaring up the UK singles chart, Kate was quoted in *Record Mirror* in February 1978; "I'm nineteen, but so what? I've had experiences too. A lot of my songs are about my own traumas. The best time for writing is when you're going though a heavy time. You have an enormous amount of energy. The best way to deal with it is not to bottle it up or take it out on someone else, but to channel it into your writing. You get ideas for songs from all sorts of situations. I just start playing the piano and the chords start telling me something. Lyrics for me just seem to go with the tune, very much hand in hand. Some lyrics take a long time to come, others just come out."

The advantages that Kate had in her formative years were not such that it would justify negating her own natural talent. Whilst the music media may have been keen to do that when Kate had shot to fame so rapidly, it is evident that she was always engaged with music from a young age. On the *The Kick Inside* promotional record, Kate said; "My other musical influences really have been things from the radio, obviously, because what you listen to are the things that are going on. And again, what my brothers were playing on the radio. At a later stage, I started seeking out my own stimulus and that came from people like Billie Holiday. She was a really important thing to happen to me. Her voice just really did things to me. So emotional and so tearing. I still can't get over how incredible her voice was and her presence. I'm into more progressive people, I guess, like David Bowie and Roxy Music and Steely Dan. I think they are a very underestimated group, especially in England. They really are an important musical influence. And nearly anything really. I love so much music. I think that's the amazing thing about it: music can go into every corner of every room. There's so many different styles of music. Everyone is great in their own right — it's just a matter of personal taste, really... I think also one of the most amazing things about music, especially for the last twenty or thirty years, is the fact that we've been able to preserve it on record. So it's no longer someone jamming in a little club in the thirties in a little smoky place. It's an eternal process. You can listen to people that have died maybe twenty years ago. You can see them on the television. You can see them moving and young. They are no longer there. You've captured that moment, purely through mechanical things, which is really quite ironic because music is such a pure emotional thing to be captured on such a mechanical modern contraption. But it's the only way we can do it."

It could be considered that in 1978, there was so much variety in popular music that it was all too easy for someone as unusual as Kate to come along and make an impact in a generally open minded musical climate. Kate was quoted in *Trouser Press* in July 1978; "Maybe it's ironic, but I think punk has actually done a lot for me in England. People were waiting for something new to come out — something with feeling. If you've got something to tell people, you should lay it on them."

The interviewer stated that as part of their conversation, Kate spoke of The Stranglers and The Sex Pistols. The late seventies was an interesting time for music because focus was just beginning to transition from rock and towards punk and new wave. The singles chart was certainly eclectic. Other popular songs at the time included Blondie's 'Denis', Bob Marley And The Wailers' 'Is This Love' and Elvis Costello's '(I Don't Want To Go To) Chelsea'. Other artists who had albums high in the charts that year included Abba, Ian Dury, and the Buzzcocks.

Still though, talent is talent and there is certainly no denying that Kate Bush had it in abundance. It was reported in the *Middlesex County Times* in March 1978; "Kate Bush, with her strange but catchy song 'Wuthering Heights', has ousted Abba from the number one position in the list of top selling records." (Abba's 'Take A Chance On Me' sat in the number two spot whilst 'Wuthering Heights' was at number one).

Notably, 'Denis' was Blondie's breakthrough single and around the same time as Kate Bush's rise to fame, Debbie Harry was also at the beginning of her own journey as a commercially successful musician. It was considered in the *Harrow Observer* in November 1979; "The recent successes of Kate Bush do seem to have persuaded the British music industry that there is a market for our own girl singers."

Kate's image as a sweet young female is certainly something that the media played on at times. In April 1978, the *Reading Evening Post* reported on the fact that Kate "had an unusual travelling companion when she flew into Heathrow Airport yesterday on her return from a visit to New York — a large Pink Panther toy. Appropriately, Kate has named him Heathcliff." And on balance, how many male musicians have seen their mums interviewed in the media? Kate Bush's mum was quoted in the *Newcastle Evening Chronicle* in October 1978; "Of course I worry about Kate at times, what mother wouldn't? But she's a very stable girl and always seems to know what she's doing. She hasn't become affected in the slightest."

It is a possibility that Kate Bush's originality could have been just as much a disadvantage as it was ultimately an advantage. Commercially, record companies and the music industry operated in a very formulaic way by the late seventies. On the promotional record for *The Kick Inside* in 1978, Kate said; "I think probably one of the most amazing things about the music scene today is the fact that music is purely one aspect of it. It is in fact a very large commercial business. This is why it is so hard for new unknown people to get into — because it's a money-making business. A lot of companies are into creating formulas that will actually make the money for them and it's hard for people who have got something new to get through. But then again, there are the people in the companies who are aware of this and I think that that's where the magic lies because if you get through to them then you're all right…

"For me, the most important thing is my music. That's what I'm here for. I think it's important that you realise that it is a business because you can't just play your music and shut yourself away because you have to communicate with your audience because they're the people that you're doing it for. You just have to comply with all the rules… I think an interesting thing is happening in the music scene at the moment — I think from the beginning of this year, especially in England. It was purely because of punk. It was a very quick dynamic thing that happened and I think its purpose was in order to bring new things out of it. We now have a sort of thing called new wave, which has come from punk, but it's not like punk at all. It's rich in interesting lyrics — a completely different attitude towards music. There are very interesting lyrics that are based a lot more on reality than a lot of things that have gone before. I think that's the trouble with a lot of music that was happening: things were becoming purely romantic bubblegum. Just talking about boy meets girl. The great thing about music is that it's a message. You actually have the power to convey a message to people to let them know about something they didn't know about before. I think that's an incredible responsibility on behalf of the artist. I find myself very aware of that and I often wonder if I am doing any good, but I know it's my purpose. It's what I must do."

'Wuthering Heights' is characterised by enchantingly melodic piano lines with strings and electric guitars backing up a memorable vocal line. Kate's high voice is unique but it's not without lower tones. The quirky nature of the song — combined with Kate's young age and attractive appearance — was such that it was very easy for the UK media to write her off as a novelty and at times, merely a sex symbol. Kate was quoted in *Tune In* in December 1978; "It's a bit of a conflict. I want to come across in an attractive way, naturally, to attract attention, but I also want to say something in the photograph. It's just very hard to draw the line between being attractive and being sexy. Naturally, looks can help, but if you can't provide something interesting to listen to, that won't hold anyone's interest for long."

Kate's image, as construed and promoted by the media, was one that she herself was keen to question in interviews. She was quoted in the *Reading Evening Post* in April 1979; "I find lots of men are intimidated by me, and I must admit I'm very intrigued by the way some women exert power over men, but I think that's just wrong. I could make my act a lot sexier than it is — do the whole female thing and become a sex object. But I'm not going to fall into that trap. It's so dangerous to come on all sexual, because you are immediately labelled as a woman instead of simply as an artist, and if I do succeed, I want to know that I made it on talent, not merely as a female female (sic)."

Superpop reported in February 1979; "With her meteoric rise to fame and fortune has come problems aplenty for her record company. She is (luckily for EMI) highly identifiable, but any attempts to promote her as a sex symbol have been politely foiled by Kate herself who keeps a careful eye on all her company's publicity campaigns. She is, it seems, determined to succeed on her musical merits alone — although she admits that some photos and posters of herself do have an erotic appeal." Kate was quoted in the same feature; "That's a very obvious image, I suppose some pictures of me are reasonably sexy but I think the true vibe from my face is there. I'm anxious to avoid being projected as a sex symbol because it distracts from my music."

As Kate's career developed she would prove herself to be a versatile artist who had more to offer than the iconic hit that resulted in her rising to fame in 1978. However, that's not to say that the iconic nature of 'Wuthering Heights' and indeed, *The Kick Inside*, was regarded as primitive and merely novel by everyone, far from it in fact.

The role of the piano is essential across the entirety of *The Kick Inside*. It is so often at the forefront of the arrangements; from the beginning of 'Wuthering Heights', it is the piano that makes such a distinctive contribution. Kate said; "The way I've always worked is to be with the piano. I never write songs without the piano — it's always me and it and we communicate. And I always write the words with the tune — they seem to come together and it's very much a thing of moods. If the chord I'm playing is telling me something, then the words will come from that. If it is a minor feel, it will be a sad song because minor chords are very sad things. If it's a major chord, it will be a slightly maybe, rockier, happier song… What happens is that I sit down and I start playing the piano and it's the progression of chords that comes out that actually leads to the song. Until I sit down at the piano I have no idea what's going to happen. Sometimes, before I go there, maybe I'll have an idea that I've picked up from a film or just from talking to someone about something I've never known about before. You can find inspiration can click in so many different ways: it can be something completely out of the blue that you'll suddenly think 'I really want to write a song.' I think that's how it works though. I think art is about spontaneous feelings and feedback of people, objects, whatever. It's just a continuous process of creation."

Kate was drawn to the piano as her instrument of choice from a young age. Paddy Bush was quoted in *Musician* in 1985; "Our mother is Irish and I think Kate maybe felt, you know, that there was a slight obligation to appease the Irish spirit. And somewhere out of my mother's imagination came the idea that Kate should learn the violin. It seems to be a tradition that the violin is forced upon people. I mean, there are few who take it up of their own volition! And Kate was certainly one of those who only took it up under pressure, she didn't really like it very much. So the piano was a kind of way of exploring music in dimensions diametrically opposite to what the violin must have represented to her. Escapism, pure escapism! You know, the command would be, 'Go and practise on that violin, Kate,' but the piano music came out instead! I think perhaps we Bushes are a bit like that... So yes, her piano playing was in the first place a direct reaction to straight music as we knew it, or as she knew it, at the time. The sort of style which she evolved in her piano playing and singing were direct opposites of all the kinds of straight music which she was being fed right then.

Pure escapism, and very beautiful!"

Kate was quoted in the *Reading Evening Post* in April 1979; "It's almost like a person to me. We have a real relationship, the piano and I. And as soon as I touch the keys, strange things happen to me. I go into a kind of trance. It's almost as though I'm travelling through time."

SOULFUL, SENSITIVE, salubrious. So why all the fuss about Kate Bush' age? Is it the fact that you don't usually get such cohesive intelligence from 19 year old females? Is it that 'child' prodigies are out of our mode? Or is it simply the fact that the journalists are getting older? It wasn't *that* long ago that the charts were brimmed from 1 to 10 with teen-aged stars. It may *seem* that only yesterday she was your average unknown person, but in fact, Kate has been developing her unique talents on rinky-dink second hand pianos since she was the ripe old age of 14. Recently she moved into a three storey flat in Lewisham, which is owned by her general practiouer daddy-o, and whose other two storeys are occupied by her two older brothers.

The story is not at all as overnight as it seems to be. It was in fact two years ago that Pink Floyd's Dave Gilmour hopped around to Kates flat with a Revox — goal in mind to get some of Kates tunes published. She wasn't, at the time, considered a singer but Gilmour, who is genuinely interested in giving undiscovered talent a shot-in-the-arm (with his Unicorn organisation) felt that the bubbling under songs should have the opportunity to be heard. They recorded about 15 songs per tape, and took them around to various record companies. The unanimous opinion, then, was 'non-commercial', and after all . . . it's not creative unless it *sells*, 'eh?

How Kate and Gilmour hooked up is rather a vague 'girlfriends'-boyfriends'-girlfriends-friend' sort of rigamaroll, but the fact is that he never did lose interest in her er . . . talents, and decided that the only way to reach a record company's goldlined pocket was to produce finished product. Which is exactly what they did. Gilmour put up the money, and Kate went into Air studios complete with a band, and laid down the three tracks she and Dave both felt were best. This is the tape which eventually landed Kate her contract with EMI Records.

Despite the fact that she has been already wrongly built (no pun intended) in the media to be a mere child, she is surprisingly aware of what is going on around her, and is accepting the entire shindig with a pleased air of disbelief.

"They keep telling me the chart numbers, and I just kind of say, 'Wow' (she sweeps her arms) . . . it's not really like it's happening. I've always been on the outside, watching albums I like go up the charts, and feeling pleased that they are doing well, but it's hard to relate to the fact that it's now happening to *me* . . ."

WUTHERING Heights', Kates' self-penned song, inspired by the book of the same title, is literally catapaulting up the UK charts, and looks as though it will be one of those classic world-wide smasherooies, though it has yet to be released to most other countries. She recently took her first air-bourne flight to Germany for a television appearance, as the single, apparently, has been chosen as whatever the German equivalent of 'pick-of-the-week' might be.

"It was mind blowing," she said euphorically, in reference to flying. "I *really* want to do more of that . . ." Wonder how she'll feel about in in two years time.

She writes songs about love, people, relationships and life . . . sincerely and emotionally, but without prostituting her talents by whining about broken hearts.

"If you're writing a song, assuming people are going to listen, then you have a responsibility to those peope. It's important to give them a positive message, something that can advise or help is far more effective than having a wank and being self-pitiful. *That's* really negative. My friends and brothers

PIX: JIL   URMANOVSKY

You don't have to be beautiful...

. . . to get your face in SOUNDS, a top twenty album and a top five single are usually enough. Fortunately Kate Bush has both, so you can't call us sexist

have been really helpful to me, providing me with stimulating conversation and ideas I can really sink my teeth into."

For as long as she can remember she has been toying around with the piano, much, I reckoned, to her parent's chargrin. Can *you* imagine living with a nine-year-old who insisted on battering away on said instrument, wailing away at the top of her lungs in accompaniment?

"Well, they weren't very encouraging in the beginning, they thought it was a lot of noise. When I first started, my voice was terrible, but the voice is an instrument to a singer, and the only way to improve it is to practise. I have had no formal vocal training, though there was a guy that I used to see for half-an-hour once a week, and he would advise me on things like breathing properly, which is very important to voice control. 'He'd say things like 'Does that hurt? Well, then sing more from here (motions to diaphram) than from your throat.' I don't like the idea of 'formal' training, it has far too many rules and conventions that are later hard to break out of . . ."

IT IS QUITE obvious from the cover of 'The Kick Inside', her debut album, that Ms. Bush is Orientally influenced, but apparently it was not meant to take on such an oriental feel.

"I think it went a bit over the top, actually. We had the kite, and as there is a song on the album by that name, and as the kite is traditionally oriental, we painted the dragon on. But I think the lettering was just a bit too much. No matter. On the whole I was surprised at the amount of control I actually had with the album production. Though I didn't choose the musicians," (Andrew Powell,

producer and arranger did). "I thought they were terrific.

"I was lucky to be able to express myself as much as I did, especially with this being a debut album. Andrew was really into working together, rather than pushing everyone around. I basically chose which tracks went on, put harmonies where I wanted them . . . I was there throughout the entire mix. I feel that's very important. Ideally, I would like to learn enough of the technical side of things to be able to produce my own stuff eventually."

Kate has a habit of gesturing constantly with her hands, and often expressing herself with unspellable sounds and grimaces. Though this make type transcriptions difficult, it does accentuate something which is very much a part of her, 'movement expression'. She has studied under the inimitable Lindsay Kemp, mime artiste, an experience shared with Kate's favourite musician, David Bowie.

"I admire actresses and actors terribly and think it's an amazing craft. But singing and performing your songs should be the same thing. At this point I would rather develope my music and expressing it physically, as opposed to having a script. I think I'm much better off as a wailer . . ."

She is, indeed a beautiful woman. Carved ivory, with nary a nick. So obviously there is no way she can avoid becoming the target for sexist minds. Although she does not advocate this reaction, she's not flustered by it. After all, it *is* a compliment.

"As long as it does not interfere with my progress as a singer/songwriter, it doesn't matter. I just wish people would think of that first, I would be foolish to think that people don't look. I suppose in some ways it helps to get more people to listen . . ."

THE KICK Inside' suggests a keen interest in mysticism. "I try to work on myself spiritually, and am always trying to improve my outlook on life. We really abuse all that we've got, assuming that we are so superior as beings, taking the liberties of sticking up cement stuff all over the place. I think there is a lot to astrology, and the effect the moon has upon us all, but I hate the way it's become so trendy now.

"I'm a vegetarian, and now that's trendy as well . . . but what annoys me the most is the way people are so automistically cynical about astrology. I mean, like the Greeks put an incredible amount of hard work into carefully planned geometric charts, based purely on mathematics. People just shrug off. It's the same with coincidence, as I said in the song 'Strange Phenomene'.

At first, Kate was opposed to having any sort of management, feeling strongly that less mistakes are made if you deal with situations yourself, directly. But she quickly found out that this sort of idealism does not work, and now has Peter Lynter-Todd handling her business affairs.

"He has worked more on the theatrical side of entertainment than music, I like that. I think most managers are crooks, greedy and non-musical, and that mixing with other music managers is contagious. I think Peter will be amazing . . ."

There are tentative plans for a Kate Bush tour in the late spring, but it is only being discussed at this point.

To accompany Kate on the road will be Conan drummer Sergio Castillo; guitarist Brian Bath; bassist Del Palmer; keyboardist Ben Barson, and brother Paddy Bush on mandolin and backing vocals. Again, primarily friends of friends of friends, and wide-eyed optimism.

JUST AS I'M about to leave a pile of fan mail arrives, and she gapes, amazed, "Cor . . . is all this for me??? This is amazing!"

Oh, dear, dear, Kate. Do stay above it all. Don't ever fall into your very own lyrics, which could be ironically revised. From 'Kite':

"I got no limbs, I'm like a feather on the wind.
Well, I'm not sure if I want to be up here at all.
And I'd like to be back on the ground."

DONNA McALLISTER

Chapter Two

The Making Of The Kick Inside

Many of the thirteen songs on *The Kick Inside* had been penned before it was time to go into the studio. In promotion for the album she said; "I do love singing other people's songs. I have done, but I feel that that is in fact cheating because there are so many good singers around who sing other people's songs and there aren't as many songwriters in comparison. For me, my only reason I sing is because I write the songs and I feel because I've written them and I know what they're about, I'm the one who can convey the message the best. But, I don't really consider myself a singer. I'm a singer/songwriter, but only because I write the songs."

Overall though, Kate's talent was in both writing and singing. In an interview with BBC Radio in 1979, she said; "I love songwriting, but I love singing even more, sometimes, you know. It's just such a pleasure to be able to open your mouth and just let it all out, it's fantastic. I don't think I could ever stop doing that."

The production featured input from several progressive rock veterans, including Duncan Mackay (whose other projects include Steve Harley & Cockney Rebel, The Alan Parsons Project, 10cc, Camel, and Budgie), Ian Bairnson, (also of The Alan Parsons Project), David Paton (of Pilot fame who was also in The Alan Parsons Project and Camel), and Stuart Elliott (Steve Harley & Cockney Rebel, The Alan Parsons Project), and of course, Dave Gilmour.

Overall, the talent of the musicians involved in *The Kick Inside* made for an album that went way beyond sounding sterile. Recording engineer Jon Kelly was quoted in *Sound On Sound* in June 2004; "I can't remember doing any editing on Kate's sessions, but I can remember 'Wuthering Heights' being a performance-y type song. Stuart was a brilliant drummer, he absolutely adored Kate's songs, and the all-round enthusiasm and will to play well on those sessions was just fantastic. They were great musicians, and everything they did was of a very high standard."

Not only was *The Kick Inside* a debut for Kate Bush; it was also the first major project for Kelly. He had previously worked on making jingles, something that he considered aided his speed in the studio for when it came to working on *The Kick Inside*. Kelly had already worked with Andrew Powell on various smaller projects.

The Kick Inside was produced by Andrew Powell and engineered by Kelly at the spacious AIR Studio Two, using the in-house twenty-four track tape machine. Studio One was used to record the string sessions in. Jon Kelly was quoted in *Sound On Sound* in June 2004 as he explained how he was "learning as I went along and dreadfully insecure. I give full credit to Andrew (Powell) and the great musicians, who were very supportive, while Kate herself was just fantastic. Looking back, she was incredible and such an inspiration, even though when she first walked in I probably thought she was just another new artist. Her openness, her enthusiasm, her obvious talent — I remember finishing that first day, having recorded two or three backing tracks, and thinking 'My God, that's it. I've peaked!'… Kate always recorded live vocals, and they were fantastic, but then she'd want to redo them later. In the case of 'Wuthering Heights', she was imitating this witch, the mad lady from the Yorkshire Moors, and she was very theatrical about it. She was such a mesmerising performer — she threw her heart and soul into everything she did — that it was difficult to ever fault her or say, 'You could do better'."

It seems that everyone who worked on *The Kick Inside* had a good working rapport. Kate was quoted in *Musician* in 1985; "The first album was all down to the producer, Andrew Powell, and the engineer, Jon Kelly. As far as I know, it was mainly Andrew Powell who chose the musicians, he'd worked with them before and they were all sort of tied in with Alan Parsons. And, on that first album, I had no say, so I was very lucky really to be given such good musicians to start with. And they were lovely, because they were all very concerned about what I thought of the treatment of each of the songs. And if I was unhappy with anything, they were more than willing to redo their parts. So they were very concerned about what I thought, which was very nice. And they were really nice guys, eager to know what the songs were about and all that sort of thing. I don't honestly see how anyone can play with feeling unless you know what the song is about. You know, you might be feeling this really positive vibe, yet the song might be something weird and heavy and sad. So I think that's always been very important for me, to sit down and tell the musicians what the song is about."

Jon Kelly said; "Kate would certainly get involved, poking her head all around to see where it sounded nice. There was a good feeling of camaraderie, so I never felt nervous, just insecure! I recorded the celeste with a Coles ribbon mic positioned on the soundboard at the back, and that worked out fine. You couldn't keep Kate away from her sessions even if you had wild dogs and bazookas. She was just drinking it all up, learning everything that went on. The first moment she walked into the control room, I could tell that's where she wanted to be, in control of her own records. She was so astute and intelligent, and she was also phenomenally easy to work with. An absolute joy. I can't remember any bad moments at all… She was the shining light of the entire sessions. You couldn't deny her anything."

Two of the songs for the album were already in the bag. "Maybe another interesting thing about this album is that two of the tracks, 'The Man With The Child In His Eyes' and 'The Saxophone Song' were recorded about three years ago," said Kate. "This was in fact my initial plunge into the business, as they say, with the help of Dave Gilmour from Pink Floyd. I managed to get through to him through a contact of my brother's and at that time he was looking around for unknown talent. He came along and heard me and we put some things down and he put up the money for me to make my first demo in a proper recording studio with arrangements. I owe to him the fact that I got my contract and that I'm where I am now. Two of these original tracks that we had on the demo are on the album, so maybe that helps with the variation."

With 'The Man With The Child In His Eyes' and 'The Saxophone Song' having been recorded in 1975, the majority of the tracks on *The Kick Inside* were recorded in the summer of 1977 when it was decided that Kate was ready to go into AIR Studios. (In November 1979, she wrote of 'The Saxophone Song' in the *Kate Bush Club* magazine; "The song isn't about David Bowie. I wrote it about the instrument, not the player, at a time when I really loved the sound of the saxophone — I still do. No, I don't know him personally, though I went to his Farewell To Ziggy Stardust concert and cried, and so did he.").

By the time *The Kick Inside* was released in the UK, 'Wuthering Heights' had already got to number one in the singles chart. 'The Man With The Child In His Eyes' was released as the second single for the UK market but in Japan, they had 'Moving' followed by 'Them Heavy People' whilst Brazil followed up 'Wuthering Heights' a year later with 'Strange Phenomena' as a single. (In a 1978 interview for Japanese TV,

Kate Bush said of 'Moving'; "I actually wrote the song for my teacher, Lindsay Kemp. But the inspiration came from whales, the big fish, you know. They just sing so beautifully, and that's why they are on the beginning of the track.").

Although in many interviews Kate has asserted that she isn't a pub singer and has never been keen on touring, in the early days, she toured pubs with the KT Bush Band. Her brother, Paddy Bush, formed the band with his friends Vic King, Brian Bath and Del Palmer. With Kate as the vocalist, they had first performed at the Rose Of Lee in Lewisham. For *The Kick Inside* though, Kate was advised to use established session musicians. As a result, Paddy Bush was the only musician from the KT Bush band to play on the album.

"I think one of the really interesting things was to compare live work with actually recording," said Kate at the time. "It's such a completely different process, because when you're gigging, which I did for a little while with my band, the KT Bush Band, we were just doing pubs around London. We were singing other peoples' songs — rock 'n' roll songs. It's really different because you feed off the audience. You can see their faces. You can tell if they hate you or if they love you. All you're trying to do when you're on the stage is to excite them, get them to have a good time and enjoy it. With the album, it's a very different thing because that's a piece of plastic that people, hopefully, will listen to again and again. So you have to make it a very different kind of thing, it has to be purely for the ear, to allow people's imaginations to just move on their own. We just tried to do this by the arrangements and harmonies. There are so many of those things that you can't do live because you, obviously, can't overdub your own voice three times when you're singing live. You can't put harmonies in — you get other people to do it… The thing actually about playing it live is that in fact we weren't doing any of my songs — we were just doing other people's rock 'n' roll numbers, because in fact, in the pubs in London, unless you're well known that's the only way you get people to listen to you. They need to know the songs and they need to be able to drink their beer and dance. And with the album, I was trying to initiate my songs, which is a completely different thing, and I was amazed at how lucky I was getting people to listen to me. I've been very lucky."

The live rhythm section on 'Wuthering Heights' included Kate playing a Bösendorfer grand piano. Stuart Elliott played drums, Andrew Powell was on bass and Ian Bairnson played a six-string acoustic. In later years, Kelly asserted that he regretted not mixing Ian Bairnson's guitar solo to be just a touch louder. Kelly was quoted in *Sound On Sound* in June 2004; "I always used to apologise to him whenever I saw him afterwards." Still though, to the untrained ear, the guitar solo still soars beautifully with everything else on 'Wuthering Heights'.

The range of instrumentation on *The Kick Inside* was such that it took some thought in terms of how best to position the mics in the studio. Predominantly, Jon Kelly stayed loyal to the setup that had been originally used by Geoff Emerick for the recording of 'The Man With The Child In His Eyes' and 'The Saxophone Song'.

Kelly recalled; "For the drums I used a D19 on the snare, Sennheiser 421s on the toms, a D12 on the bass drum and a (Neumann) KM84 on the hi-hat. The bass was DI'd and amped — at the time I was very keen on the Susan Blue DI box, while a Marshall cabinet and Marshall head were mic'd with an FET 47. Ian Bairnson's acoustic was recorded with a Neumann U87, as were Kate's piano and vocal — I was a big 87 fan, I used to use them on everything. I still think it's a really underrated microphone. When people listen to one on its own they often think it's a bit hard and doesn't have such a huge sound as some of the valve or softer-focus mics, but it's so efficient once you place it within the mix." (I recognise that this quote contains a lot of jargon but I've included it here on the basis that it may be of interest to some).

Dave Paton was predominantly the bassist on *The Kick Inside* but on 'Wuthering Heights' he overdubbed with a 12-string acoustic guitar. This was double tracked in order to create a sense of depth and atmosphere. Andrew Powell hired the celeste. It was used to double with the piano arpeggios that feature on the song's famous introduction. The same combination features on the small sections leading into the chorus. Percussionist Morris Pert was next to do some overdubs. He spent a day working on *The Kick Inside*.

"The only things he played on 'Wuthering Heights' were crotals, which are like disc-shaped glockenspiels," said Kelly. "Again, these were doubled with the piano motif throughout the song."

The strings recorded in AIR's Studio One consisted of eight first violins, six second violins, six violas and six cellos. There were also three French horns. All of the latter feature on 'Wuthering Heights'. In the instance of other songs on *The Kick Inside*, a smaller selection of instrumentation was used. The parts for a few other tracks on the album were recorded in sessions that lasted three hours at a time.

Kelly recalled; "That was a huge room, twice as big as the live area in Studio Two. It could accommodate between sixty to seventy musicians, and had high ceilings and a lovely, bright sound. Everything sounded great in there. I mic'd the first violins with a couple of 87s, as I did for the second violins, the violas, the French horns and overheads — back then you could have called me Mr 87. At least there were FET 47s on the cellos. I'd try to use as few mics as possible in Studio One because the room sounded so good and there was this phase thing going on — the more mics you used, you could fool yourself into thinking it sounded better, but things would cancel one another out and you'd lose the vibrancy. Nothing was slaved, everything was kept 24-track on this album, and that was fortunate because slaving was a really laborious process in those days — before Q-lock enabled us to efficiently run two machines together, we'd have to physically get two tapes in the right position to start a song. Tracks one through five were hi-hat, bass drum, overhead left, overhead right and snare — hi-hat would always be the first casualty if we needed an extra track — and tracks seven and eight were the tom-toms. Track six was missed out because you couldn't pan between odd and even on the Neve desks in AIR, while some of the groups had faders on them and some weren't normalised. You had to be careful about getting groups caught between the two, because there were cancellation problems. Meanwhile, the strings were mixed to two tracks and the French horns went to just one track."

The electric guitar solo played by Ian Bairnson that features on the outro fade of 'Wuthering Heights' was played in the control room of Studio Two on a Les Paul. Jon Kelly said; "Ian warmed up and developed that solo while I got the monitoring right, and there was one take that was just great. Being in the control room, he missed the feedback from the amp, and I can remember telling him to get close to the speakers, expecting this to do the same. You can tell I was pretty naïve."

The Kick Inside was mixed in AIR's Studio Three. Not only was the album broad in terms of variety of instrumentation, but also in terms of the songs themselves. Kate said; "There are thirteen tracks on this album. When we were getting it together, one of the most important things that was on all our minds was that, because there were so many, we wanted to try and get as much variation as we could. To a certain extent, the actual songs allowed this because of the tempo changes, but there were certain songs that had to have a funky rhythm and there were others that had to be very subtle. I was very greatly helped by my producer and arranger Andrew Powell, who really is quite incredible at tuning into my songs. We made sure that there was one of the tracks, just me and the piano, to, again, give the variation. We've got a rock 'n' roll number in there, which again was important. And all the others there are just really the moods of the songs set with instruments, which for me is the most important thing, because you can so often get a beautiful song, but the arrangements can completely spoil it — they have to really work together."

The Kick Inside was originally released on LP and cassette. In this day and age of uniformity, it's extraordinary that there are seven different versions of the album's cover that were used around the world. Either way, it is the only album of Kate Bush's to have different covers for the following countries: UK, USA, Canada, Japan, Yugoslavia and Uruguay (the latter being rare and an expensive purchase for record collectors today). *The Kick Inside* had two UK releases in picture disc format, both limited editions. The record came in a full colour sleeve with a sticker to denote the fact that a picture disc was inside. Versions exist of *The Kick Inside* that were released on different coloured vinyl pressings. A grey version was available in Holland and green, pink and multicoloured were available in Czechoslovakia. The album was also released on an 8-track cartridge in Canada. *The Kick Inside* was first released on CD in Japan in 1983. It wasn't until three years later that Europe would see a CD release of the album.

Jay Myrdal did the photography for the famous UK cover. He had listened to 'Wuthering Heights' before doing the photoshoot and on account of Kate's voice being (as he perceived it!) "shrill", he didn't have high expectations for the album's commercial success. Nevertheless, he was on board with the fact that EMI anticipated that *The Kick Inside* would at least make some kind of dent in the charts. Years later, he admitted, "what do I know?"

Kate turned up for the photoshoot with wood and painted

paper. They were constructed into a kite. The fragile contraption was rigged up with ropes and a metal bar against a black painted wall of the photography studio. The whole thing was strong enough for the petite singer to hang from. The whole idea for the cover came from Kate and the art director, Steve Ridgeway. It was inspired by the scene in Disney's *Pinocchio* where Jiminy Cricket glides past the whale's eye using his umbrella as a parachute. The photo against the black wall was used on the 'Wuthering Heights' single (the UK release and the vast majority of European releases); a perfect choice considering that in the UK and indeed globally, 'Kite' was on the B-side of the single.

The back cover has an illustration of a man on a kite. It was done by Del Palmer. The sky in the background was photographed by John Carder Bush. The illustration features the KT symbol. The symbol has been used on all of Kate's album artwork since. Upon close analysis, there is also a pictogram of Del's name on the right wing of the kite. In an interview with BBC Radio in 1979, Kate was asked about the KT symbol that features on the kite on the album artwork. She explained, "That actual sign is an old Knights Templar's sign and around the countryside you'll find it scattered on the doorways of churches and things and it was just very fitting because I used to be in a band called the KT Bush Band. Katie, KT. And it's just a theme that we've kept running."

'James And The Cold Gun' had initially been considered as the debut single but Kate keenly persuaded EMI to go with 'Wuthering Heights' instead. The commercial success of 'Wuthering Heights' speaks for itself; Kate made a good choice in choosing the track and EMI did the right thing in allowing her to go with her strong feelings on the matter. Musically and artistically, it was an excellent choice for a debut single in terms of how stark and distinctive it was. 'Wuthering Heights' was worthy of attention on a large scale and arguably, the song was the making of Kate Bush and the start of an exciting and fruitful music career. It's fascinating to consider what could have been (or indeed, not been!) had 'James And The Cold Gun' been released instead of 'Wuthering Heights'. Not only was 'Wuthering Heights' a knockout song, it was a large aspect of Kate's image overall as she rose to fame in the UK.

And who was James? Kate explained in the *Kate Bush Club* magazine in November 1979; "I've had lots of letters about this, many from people called James, with plenty of suggestions for identities of the James, but the answer is: nobody. When I wrote the song, James was the right name for it."

There is so much more of an explicit story to 'Wuthering Heights' with this information in mind — all possibly important factors in terms of what it was about Kate's music that endeared people to her upon the release of her debut single. Still though, there is no denying that 'James And The Cold Gun' has plenty of strong ingredients as a song that *could* have made it work as a single; melodic hooks and belting vocals all within the safe structure of verses and chorus.

Kate was quoted in *Tune In* in December 1978; "For me, 'Wuthering Heights' was the only single and I felt very strongly about it. Eventually they agreed, but it would have been terrible if it had failed after all the effort I had put into it."

It was in September 1977 that EMI had first decided that they wanted to release 'James And The Cold Gun' as Kate's debut single but she was certain that she wanted the single to be 'Wuthering Heights'. The debut single was supposed to be released by November '77 but Kate was keen to have more work done on the album's cover art whereby she wanted the kite theme and Del Palmer's photo to be included.

Choosing to go with the young talent's enthusiasm for the song, EMI released 'Wuthering Heights' in January 1978 and it stormed the UK charts. Whilst the song had lots of success globally, it didn't make it in America. It was a good few years later that Kate would go on to crack America. In an interview with BBC Radio in 1979, she was asked about how much say she had in what was released by the record company. Her response: "Quite a lot actually. Probably more then than I am entitled to. But we discuss it. I mean, it's not really me saying 'I want this' and them going 'We want this.' We do come to a compromise in a discussion, it's quite human."

For the second single, EMI had 'Them Heavy People' in mind. However, Kate was keen to choose a song that would best showcase the fact that there was more to her than the misunderstood element of her public image. At that stage of her career in particular, there were still people who thought she was a mere novelty. Kate was quoted in the *Newcastle Evening Chronicle* in October 1978; "After the success of 'Wuthering Heights' I was worried that people would just think I was simply a squeaky voice. That single was quite bizarre in a way and I was afraid people just liked it for the novelty value rather than for the music. I think the last record, 'The Man With The Child In His Eyes', did a little to get away from that because it was in a lower key for a start. It would have been terrible if I'd had to spend the rest of my life squeaking and very sore on the tonsils, I should think."

It's not that Kate was against the idea of 'Them Heavy People' being released as a single, it was that she just didn't want it to be the *second* single. She wrote in the *Kate Bush Club* magazine in November 1979; "I always felt that 'Them Heavy People' should be a single, but I just had a feeling that it shouldn't be a second single, although a lot of people wanted that. Maybe that's why I had the feeling — because it was to happen a little later, and in fact I never really liked the album version much because it should be quite loose, you know: it's a very human song. And I think, in fact, every time I do it, it gets even looser. I've danced and sung that song so many times now, but it's still like a hymn to me when I sing it. I do sometimes get bored with the actual words I'm singing, but the meaning I put into them is still a comfort. It's like a prayer, and it reminds me of direction. And it can't help but help me when I'm singing those words. Subconsciously they must go in."

Dave Gilmour had always felt positive about the prospect of releasing 'The Man With The Child In His Eyes' as a single. This is perhaps something that may have added weight to Kate's case for releasing the song as the follow up single to 'Wuthering Heights'.

'The Man With The Child In His Eyes' was released as Kate's second single in May 1978 and it got to number six. It was reviewed in *Melody Maker* in June 1978; "A pretty song... fascinating and distinctive vocal style... lovely." It was advocated in *Sounds* in the same month; "It can't fail. She alternates between little girl voice and mental seduction... buy it — preferably for every member of your family too!" Even though not everyone was a fan of Kate Bush and her music, and even though the media sometimes still made fun, by mid 1978, it didn't necessarily matter anymore.

In July, 'The Man With The Child In His Eyes' did so well as a single that it resulted in *The Kick Inside* going back up to number eight in the UK albums chart. It was asserted in the *Liverpool Echo* in June 1978; "When I first heard 'The Man With The Child In His Eyes' on Kate Bush's debut album, *The Kick Inside*, I thought it would make an excellent if not unusual single. So it's nice to see it put out as a 45rpm this week. Kate uses her extraordinary voice to float to the top and the bottom of the scales on this tale of first love."

Kate was quoted of 'Man With The Child In His Eyes' in *Music Journal* in December 1978; "She sees this man as an all-consuming figure. He's wise, yet he retains a certain innocent quality. The song tells how his eyes give away his inner light. He's a very real character to the girl, but nobody else knows whether he really exists."

On the *The Kick Inside* promotional record Kate said; "The inspiration for 'The Man With The Child In His Eyes' was really just a particular thing that happened when I went to the piano. The piano just started speaking to me. It was a theory that I'd had for a while that I just observed in most of the men that I know: the fact that they just are little boys inside and how wonderful it is that they manage to retain this magic... I myself am attracted to older men, I guess, but I think that's the same with every female. I think it's a very natural, basic instinct that you look continually for your father for the rest of your life, as do men continually look for their mother in the women that they meet. I don't think we're all aware of it, but I think it is basically true. You look for that security in the opposite sex that your parents gave you as a child."

The child in the picture sleeve of 'The Man With The Child In His Eyes' is a photo of Kate Bush from when she was younger. She confirmed in the *Kate Bush Club* magazine in summer 1979; "the photo was taken by my brother, John."

It comes across that 'Them Heavy People' wasn't a difficult song for Kate to write. She wrote of it in the *Kate Bush Club* magazine in November 1979; "The idea for 'Them Heavy People' came when I was just sitting one day in my parent's house. I heard the phrase "rolling the ball" in my head, and I thought that it would be a good way to start a song, so I ran to the piano and played it and got the chords down. I then worked on it from there... It has lots of different people and ideas and things like that in it, and they came to me amazingly easily — it was a bit like 'Oh England' because in a way so much of it was what was happening at home at the time. My brother and my father were very much involved in talking about Gurdjieff and whirling Dervishes, and I was really getting into it too. It was just like plucking out a bit of that and putting it into something that rhymed. And it happened so easily — in a way, too easily. I say that because normally it's difficult to get it all to happen at once, but sometimes it does, and that can seem sort of wrong. Usually you have to work hard for things to happen, but it seems that the better you get at them the more likely you are to do something that is good without any effort. And because of that it's always a surprise when something comes easily. I thought it was important not to be narrow-minded just because we talked about Gurdjieff. I knew that I didn't mean his system was the only way, and that was why it was important to include whirling Dervishes and Jesus, because they are strong too. Anyway, in the long run, although somebody might be into all of them, it's really you that does it — they're just the vehicle to get you there."

Of the title track Kate said; "The song 'The Kick Inside' was inspired by a traditional folk song and it was an area that I wanted to explore because it's one that is really untouched and that is one of incest. There are so many songs about love, but they are always on such an obvious level. This song is about a brother and a sister who are in love and the sister becomes pregnant by her brother. And because it is so taboo and unheard of, she kills herself in order to preserve her brother's name in the family. The actual song is in fact the suicide note. The sister is saying 'I'm doing it for you' and 'don't worry, I'll come back to you someday.' this is it."

Kate cleverly took a folk song and remoulded it into a suicide note. In the original song, 'Lucy Wan', it is Lucy is killed by her brother when he finds out that she is pregnant with his child. Through Kate's treatment of the original material though, the character of Lucy is given a voice, perhaps even an empowerment whereby she is in charge of her own life and death.

Kate was quoted of 'The Kick Inside' in *Trouser Press* in July 1978; "It's about a young girl and her brother who fall desperately in love. It's an incredibly taboo thing. She becomes pregnant by her brother and it's completely against all morals.

She doesn't want him to be hurt, she doesn't want her family to be ashamed or disgusted, so she kills herself. The song is a suicide note."

In 1979 for a BBC Radio interview, Kate was asked, "Kate you seem very advanced in your years with some of the titles. I mean, for your first album you call it *The Kick Inside*. 'The Kick Inside' and then 'The Man With The Child In His Eyes', I mean these titles, they just come to you like that? A flash of inspiration or did you think about titles like that?" Her response was; "Well, 'The Man With The Child In His Eyes' just happened. And I think it had something to do with one of my nephew's books. I don't remember how, but that line just happened. And sometimes they just sort of get contrively (sic) written, you know what I mean? Sometimes they just happen."

Kate's videos were just as memorable as her music. In the second issue of the *Kate Bush Club* magazine in summer 1979, she wrote; "The videos seen on TV in the UK were made by Keef MacMillan, a fantastic man who I really enjoy working with, and who's now a good friend. It starts when he comes for three or four hours in an evening, and we sit and talk about what we want to do. So far, at each stage our thinking has been on the same level, which is very good. I tell him what I've got in mind, and he says that that was what he was thinking too. I then show him the routine, and he thinks of different camera angles and possible effects. Then we go into the studio and do it, and each time we've taken a whole day. His camera crew are the most amazing guys, and all work hours of overtime because they want to do it well, which is really unusual. To start with I sit and listen to the song, and think of the personality who is in it. The easiest was 'The Man With The Child In His Eyes'. I was sitting listening, trying to figure out who was singing it, and my brother John suggested I do it like that, sitting down. Then all I had to do was think about floor exercises I had done in previous lessons. I had the idea of someone sitting down and telling someone something rather secret, and put in human, rather nervous habits, like pulling hair, rubbing the nose, looking up to heaven, and that sort of thing; trying to characterise it that way. Then when I've listened once, I put the track on again and start moving, keeping on to the end. The ideas come to me with the words, and then I try to refine it. It's hard to get as much variation as I'd like, but that's a lot to do with the fact that I'm not a dancer. When we did the filming on that song, a lot of time was spent on the lighting, which was very complicated, and the Perspex box that I sat on to give a floating effect, with lights underneath, got very hot. By the end of the day I had an incredible rivet mark where I was sitting, which stayed for about four days. Every time I moved, it sounded like sandpaper. I really enjoy doing the videos, but by the end I really ache, and it gets very hot, especially under the thick makeup. But there's a nice tired feeling with a good day's work behind you. It's a real team effort, with everyone really enthusiastic and interested in helping me to enjoy it."

Kate said of the video for 'The Man With The Child In His Eyes' in a TV interview on *Razzmatazz* in 1981, "That probably was the simplest one we've ever done. Again, the song dictated it. It was a very intimate song, about a young girl almost voicing her inner thoughts, not really to anyone, but rather to herself."

By the June of 1978, Kate had already started to choose the songs for what would be her second album. The demo was made in her own studio. She was quoted in *Record Mirror* in February 1978; "I'm really not sure how I'm going to develop from now, what direction my writing will take."

The Kick Inside really was just the beginning for Kate Bush. She said; "The things that I hope for the future are that I continue to write songs and sing and that they progress. That they become more purposeful — that they have a purpose there all the time. One of the most important things to me is that I expand as a human being. So really any other sort of other levels that would take me onto a different plane, I'm welcome to if it's right. I'd love to get into the film media sometime, but I don't know if I — as an actress — can act. I don't think I could. I don't know. I'll just wait and see what comes and hope that I can expand and grow."

Jon Kelly was quoted in *Sound On Sound* in June 2004; "I love the fact that performance was our main concern back then, and that everything had a distinctly human feel. These days, that whole album would be approached differently — it might end up with a Logic sequencer somewhere — but in the final analysis, Kate's talent would shine through anything. It would shine through an old dustbin lid and a rubber band."

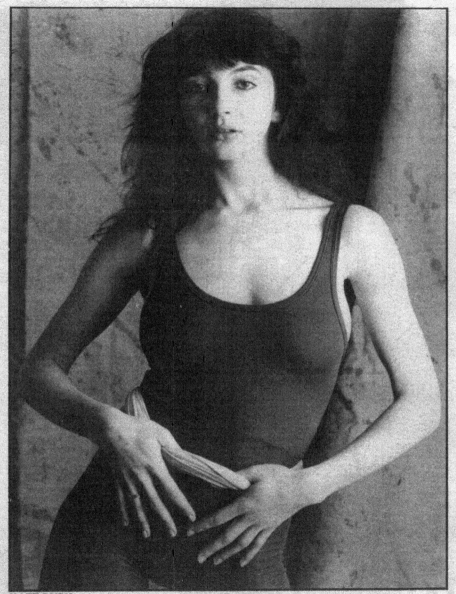

KATE BUSH

Kate Bush: one for the road

KATE BUSH, whose 'Wuthering Heights' single has risen to number 27 in this week's charts, is now rehearsing a show to take out on the road later in the spring. Kate, who comes from Welling in Kent and studied to be a dancer under Lyndsey Kemp as well as singing on the London pub circuit, has already formed a band, but names cannot be released until contracts have been settled.

Her single comes from her debut album, 'The Kick Inside', which has just been released by EMI.

One of the extraordinary facts about Kate Bush's debut album was the number of different sleeve designs around the world. Although most of the world used the design that Kate had invested her personal ideas in, there were plenty of alternatives — great for collectors!

Top: UK original
Middle: US
Bottom: Japanese

US 2nd press

Yugoslavia original

Uraguay original

Swedish tape repress

With America having opted for a different cover design, a later reissue of the album used yet another sleeve design, of Kate sat in a box! Yugoslavia went for its own unique cover of Kate in a white dress. The black and white face photo was used on the very rare version of the album pressed in Uruguay whereas a cassette reissue of the album in Sweden had a photo of Kate dancing in the white dress, probably from the same photo shoot as the one used on the Yugoslav cover.

Argentina

Canada 8-track

US 2nd press-8-track

Although Argentina used the standard album cover they added the title in Spanish.

Capitol Records also released the album on 8-track cartridge in North America. Despite the album not being a huge seller in America, 8-track cartridge was a very popular format.

Netherlands

Germany

The cassette format was very popular in the late seventies and threw up a number of variations.

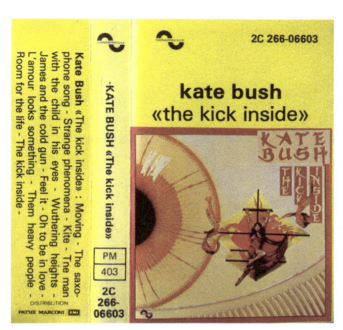

kate bush
«the kick inside»

2C 266-06603

-KATE BUSH «The kick inside»

Kate Bush «The kick inside» : Moving - The saxophone song - Strange phenomena - Kite - The man with the child in his eyes - Wuthering heights - James and the cold gun - Feel it - Oh to be in love - L'amour looks something - Them heavy people - Room for the life - The kick inside -

PM
403

2C
266-
06603

DISTRIBUTION
PATHÉ MARCONI EMI

France

EMI BRIGADIERS

DOLBY SYSTEM

THE KICK INSIDE
Kate Bush

MOVING; THE SAXOPHONE SONG; STRANGE PHENOMENA; KITE; THE MAN WITH THE CHILD IN HIS EYES; WUTHERING HEIGHTS; JAMES AND THE COLD GUN; FEEL IT; OH TO BE IN LOVE; L'AMOUR LOOKS SOMETHING LIKE YOU; THEM HEAVY PEOPLE; ROOM FOR THE LIFE; THE KICK INSIDE;

L4-
EMCJ
(N)
5131

CASSETTE STEREO KASSET

South Africa

The extraordinary success of 'Wuthering Heights' was key to boosting sales of *The Kick Inside.* The single was released in a variety of sleeve designs around the world.

UK

USA

Netherlands

Spain

Poland

Brazil

Italy

'Moving' and 'Them Heavy People' were unique Japanese single releases from the album. Elsewhere the follow up to 'Wuthering Heights' was 'The Man With The Child In His Eyes'.

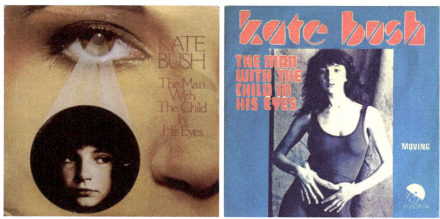

UK

Belgium

Chapter Three

Impact And Legacy

As much as Kate Bush divided opinion with her music, there were many who could see her potential based on *The Kick Inside*. In was advocated in *Trouser Press* in July 1978; "One of the best ways to look silly is to make predictions. Still, I suspect Kate Bush will have a lot of staying power. Her LP is so fully realised, and so distinctive that if her music progresses at all, she may well come to be one of those creative voices that everyone, pro and con, must take into account. Her unapologetic self-assurance never wanes and looks like the thing that will allow continued exploration."

As soon as the needle is on the record and the opening track of 'Moving' begins, you know it's going to be a journey. With whale song, soaring vocals and an alluring melody, the song makes it clear that *The Kick Inside* has the potential to be an emotional listening experience. 'Moving' was released as Kate's debut single in Japan. It went to number one there.

It was reported in the *Newcastle Journal* in June 1978 that she won the silver prize in the seventh Tokyo Song Festival with 'Moving'. Clearly a well-deserved achievement for the song in and of itself but nevertheless, it is interesting to consider that in 'Moving', the melody makes strong use of the pentatonic scale — a scale which is tremendously prevalent in both traditional and popular music in that part of the world (there is also abundant use of the pentatonic scale on 'Feel It' and in parts of 'Oh To Be In Love' and 'Wuthering Heights').

In November 1979, Kate wrote of the whale song in the

Kate Bush Club magazine; "Lots of members have written to ask what I think about whale hunting. Well, I'm dead against it. It would be a terrible tragedy if those beautiful and noble animals were wiped out by our greed."

Religion, philosophy and sex, *The Kick Inside* has it all. In an interview with BBC Radio in 1979, Kate said; "I always have to have some kind of idea of a subject matter before I start writing. Sometimes it will just come out, and sometimes it will take me days, weeks, whatever. It's very, very unpredictable and I just have to go with it, you know?... If I've got a strong idea, I'll often have a couple of lyric lines that I just fit music to and work the rest in. But normally the music comes first."

It was considered in *Trouser Press* in July 1978; "No matter if she succeeded, the album turned out to be unusual enough regardless. Bush's songs are based on simple piano chords utilised in clever variations that nag at you much the way Bryan Ferry's do. The lyrics are striking, even at a casual glance, just because they are about things (rare) and because they avoid clichés (rarer still); many tunes are about sex, but with none of the "consuming bitch" or the "submissive lady" so often in weary evidence. Instead, Kate espouses the view that sex can be fun, maybe even a good idea: '...it could be love/Or it could be just lust but it will be fun.' Other numbers concerned strange phenomena, outlaws, and Emily Brontë, but through all of it came a loopy immediacy that distanced Kate from your average creaky balladeer."

In response to the question of "In 'Them Heavy People' you mention Gurdjieff: Do you follow his teachings?" Kate wrote in the *Kate Bush Club* magazine in November 1979; "I've read some of his work, and recently saw the film *Meetings With Remarkable Men*, and had tea with Peter Brook, the director, afterwards. Pa and my brother John are into him seriously, and I'm hoping to persuade John to write an article about him for a future newsletter."

In *Trouser Press* in July 1978, Kate was quoted as describing Gurdjieff as "the only religion I've been able to relate to... I don't really want to say much because I don't really have the knowledge to say it." In an interview with BBC Radio in 1982, Kate elaborated, "Gurdjieff was really an influence in that I'd just read some of his books and really no more than that. And I'd just found a lot of what he said interesting, but that's really as far as it goes... Gurdjieff — he was considered a leader of a religious movement, I think. But as far as I know he just had a lot of ideas about creating a way that would make people stronger and more together. And it's just a different way of doing it. And it was also trying to go for a more western way of doing. But I do very little about it, so I really wouldn't like to say very much because it's a subject that I feel if I'm going to speak about then I should know what I'm talking about and I don't."

"It's all about the coincidences that happen to all of us, all of the time. Like maybe you're listening to the radio and a certain thing will come up, you go outside and it will happen again," said Kate of the track 'Strange Phenomena'. "It's just how similar things seem to attract together. Like the saying 'birds of a feather flock together' and how these things do happen to us all the time. Just strange coincidences that we're only occasionally aware of. And maybe you'll think how strange that is, but it happens all the time."

In an interview with BBC Radio in 1979, Kate said; "I guess I'm pretty pleased with 'Strange Phenomena'... It's all about coincidences. And there's in fact a school of thought about that called, well, it's synchronicity. And it's about all the things that happen that are very similar and how one day all these really strange coincidences will happen to you. And a lot of these happen to me. Like I'll be talking about something to someone and I'll go home and someone will ring me up about the same thing. And I think it's one of our phenomena's, I must admit, yeah… Well they do happen a lot, like just being in places and someone you haven't seen for years will turn up. Reading a book and seeing it in a shop and then seeing it on a bus. They happen all the time, and it happens to everyone. I mean, people are full of these little things that happen to them."

Upon being asked whether the lyrics in 'Strange Phenomena' were suggestive that she believed in other forces, Kate was quoted in *Trouser Press* in July 1978; "Oh yes, I do. The thing about us humans is that we consider ourselves it, that we know everything. I think we're abusing our power and are guided by things we don't know about that are much stronger than us. But you can't label them if you don't know what they are. Also, it tends to sound a bit trendy like "the cosmic forces" and it's cruel to do that because most religions have been exploited. As long as they're not misinterpreted they're good because they give the individual something to hold onto."

In an interview with BBC Radio in 1979, Kate was asked what the lyrics "Om mani padme hum" mean. Her response: "Well, it's a Buddhist chant actually, and I couldn't actually tell you what it means because unfortunately I don't practice Buddhism. But it's a passion mantra, and it's really just a meditative chant that people use when they're in a state of higher being."

For all of the meaning in her lyrics, there is plenty of ambiguity too. In the *Kate Bush Club* magazine in April 1980, Kate was asked, "In 'Strange Phenomena' you sing 'G arrives.' Who or what is 'G'?" Her response: "G is in fact someone we know called Mr G."

The range of subject matters explored on *The Kick Inside* resulted in Kate being asked some fascinating questions. In an interview with the *New Zealand Listener* in December 1978, Kate was asked if she had an interest in the occult based on some of her lyrics. The interviewer referred to the "whirling of the dervishes" (from 'Them Heavy People'), Beelzebub (from 'Kite') and "let me grab your soul" (from 'Wuthering Heights'). Kate was quoted; "That's really interesting, that's an amazing thing about interviews, they really make you think. I am interested in the occult but not the negative side of it. I really don't know much about it. I believe we are controlled by forces — the moon and the stars."

In an interview with BBC Radio in 1979, Kate said; "Sometimes in the recording studio, when you're out there alone, with all the lights dim, you sort of feel very strange things sometimes. That can be quite eerie. You sometimes feel that maybe there's someone in the room with you, that sort of thing. But I haven't really had anything extremely eerie or horrible happen to me. I've had quite a nice life, actually... I don't think I'm psychic, but I think I have a slight advantage being a female to start with — I'm not saying they're more sensitive, but they just seem to be more open to certain areas like that. And I do get very strong feelings sometimes that do turn out to be true, just feelings about friends, relatives, that sort of thing. But I think everyone gets them... Sometimes in dreams, but sometimes just feelings, when you're sitting down and you suddenly think about someone. Something wrong, and you give them a ring and there it is... It doesn't happen much, but I think it happens to everyone. Everyone I know has had very similar experiences... I think there's a lot in astrology. I think it's a very ancient, well mathematically planned out thing that a lot of people boo-hoo. And I think it's very unfair, because there's a lot of very strong, scientific knowledge in there. I think it's been commercialised a lot, which is why people become so cynical. But I think the fact that people are born at a certain time, on a certain day, with stars in certain positions, is bound to have some effect on that person because we are ruled by everything around us... I have what I call my own religion. I think everyone's got their own religion. There are various certain things I stick by... such as not eating meat.

Such as trying to be aware of people around me and doing my work and trying to be positive about it. I think being positive is very important… I think certainly this life at the moment is all we're living — I don't see how anyone can really say what happens when our body dies. I mean there's no way of proving where the energy goes. I hope one day they'll be able to tap it."

The Kick Inside was reviewed in *Record Mirror* in February 1978; "She fits snugly nowhere. Kate needs a new file… 'Wuthering Heights' is special, too special for anything else on *The Kick Inside* to equal. The album is quite normal — normal, but not ordinary… The sophistication is tremendous for anyone, incredible for a teenager… she is a find, a precious asset… Where did she spring from? And where to? I'm watching."

It was reviewed in *Sounds* in the same month; "What is this supposed to be? Doom-laden, "meaningful" songs (with some of the worst lyrics ever) sung with the most irritatingly yelping voice since Robert Plant… How can they persist with this redundant tax loss stuff?"

And in *New Musical Express*; "Many of the songs are ordinary, constructed in identical fashion… The relative novelty of her approach guarantees interest… 'Wuthering Heights' is utterly mesmeric… the album seems more a product of 1968 than 1978 with its smatterings of orientalism and mysticism… It's a bewildering record. While sometimes it just seems pathetically contrived, at others it suggests that there's talent trying to get out. Should the name Kate Bush resume its former anonymity in a few month's time, this album will be guaranteed a cult following in years ahead. I think it more likely that she'll make albums that are infinitely better than this one."

The reviewer made an interesting point about the idea that *The Kick Inside* could pass for something that was made in the late sixties. They're possibly not wrong; it is very trippy and experimental and of course, that's not a bad thing for people who enjoy that sort of thing. And the orientalism and mysticism?

Well, that's largely part of the character of the album, and an enchanting one at that.

The debut album was reviewed in *Melody Maker* in March 1978; "*The Kick Inside* is not a great album, but there are occasional flashes of brilliance that make me shudder when I think of her future... *The Kick Inside* may not be a great album. On the basis of the first side it just about makes it a good one, but Kate Bush could have a great future."

It was reviewed in *Hot Press* in the same month; "She possesses a remarkable talent... which isn't to claim that *The Kick Inside* will go anywhere near ranking among the best albums of 1978, it probably won't. But as an initial statement from a nineteen-year-old singer and songwriter, quite simply it unveils a potential that's almost frightening... Kate Bush could make great albums given time."

By the beginning of April 1978, 'Wuthering Heights' was coming back down the UK singles chart after reaching its peak. *The Kick Inside* was also coming down from a similar height. It was during this time that Kate had a lot of international interest in her music. Although she was yet to crack the US, she had fans in Europe, Canada, Australia and South America. It was reported in *Music Journal* in December 1978; "Released in the US several months ago, Kate's album, *The Kick Inside*, has not achieved overwhelming success in the States as of yet, but that may soon change. The album has been reissued with a new album cover, and impressive AOR radio support has been building for Kate's remarkable music. Almost every cut on the debut record is equal to, or even better than, 'Wuthering Heights'... Appearances on European television programs like *Top Of The Pops*, *Saturday Night At The Mill* and *Tonight* helped launch Bush, still new to performing, into a sudden spotlight — and more than a little controversy. Her act is a sensual combination of dance and dramatic vocal presentations, her body not exactly hidden in a flesh-coloured body stocking, and some viewers apparently found Kate to be erotically shocking or in bad taste. Even Kate cringes at the thought of those first, unpractised attempts at visual communication... With or without the sensationalism surrounding her good looks and offbeat performing style, Kate writes music of incredible depth. Just as her dawning public image comes up displaying the physical woman, so do her amazing lyrics bespeak one hundred percent twentieth century female. Seldom, if ever, has the feminine standpoint been more boldly and beautifully stated, and songs like 'Room For The Life', 'Strange Phenomena' or 'Feel It' penetrate directly to new depths of corporeal and spiritual realisation... Some of the poetry herein is unexpurgated and erotic, other portions take an inanimate pose to evoke new feelings from the listener... Perhaps 'Wuthering Heights' could only scale the pop music charts in her native England, fuelled by fervour for the great British novel, and novelty. Maybe America's top forty isn't quite ready for a singer-poet-pianist this unusual and challenging, even if she has sold over 250,000 albums in the smallish UK. But we're all going to find out. Kate Bush is demonstrating the kind of creative imagination and insight that could have an impact on music now and for years to come".

Efforts were made to get through to America with *The Kick Inside*. An EMI press release for America stated:

Kate Bush: "One day, along comes this friend of my brother's. He worked in the record business himself and thought he might be able to make contacts. Well, he knew Pink Floyd from Cambridge and he asked Dave Gilmour (Pink Floyd's guitarist) down to hear me."

Little did Dave Gilmour know that he was about to meet the child-woman who, only a scant two years later, would have the number one hit in England with her single debut

'Wuthering Heights'.

'Wuthering Heights' is an eerie, almost hypnotic tune which is based on the section of Emily Bronte's novel where Cathy Earnshaw wants to seize Heathcliff's soul so they can be together in the spirit world; on the surface an unlikely candidate for pop chart success. It's a measure of Bush's right instincts and the charisma of her talent that the single became such a huge success and won column after column of critic's raves in the English press.

"When I first read Wuthering Heights, I thought the story was so strong. This young girl in an era when the female role was so inferior and she was coming out with this passionate, heavy stuff. Great subject matter for a song. I loved writing it," she enthuses, "it was a real challenge to perceive the whole mood of a book into such a short piece of prose. Also, when I was a child I was always called Cathy not Kate and I just found myself able to relate to her as a character. It's so important to put yourself in the role of the person in a song. There's no half measure. When I sing that song I am Cathy."

'Wuthering Heights' was only a harbinger of things to come from the talented Kate Bush. With the release of her debut EMI America album, The Kick Inside (previously released in North America by Capitol in March 1978), Kate Bush herself is rapidly on the way to becoming a classic in her own time. (The LP earned the nineteen year old singer/ songwriter top ten honours on the British pop charts prior to its US release.)

Born July 30, 1958, she grew up in Plumstead in Kent, England, and seemed destined from an early age to become involved with music.

"I have two older brothers and they were very keen on musical instruments. So I just grew up with music all around me," she explains, "when I was about eleven I just started poking around at the piano and started making up little songs. I never played Beatles songs or anything like that. I was always just exploring the instrument. Then, when I was fourteen, I started taking it seriously and I began to treat the words to the songs as poetry. I'd always been keen on poetry at school and it was lovely to put the poems together with the music."

Then, along came Dave Gilmour. Impressed by her talent he funded a session at the AIR London studios for Bush to record a demo tape. EMI heard the tape and signed Kate Bush to the label, post haste. Because she was so young (sixteen at the time), it was decided that she should spend the next few years developing her already considerable talents.

She studied mime and modern dance with the highly respected Lindsay Kemp (who also tutored David Bowie) for a short time. After Kemp went to Australia, Bush began dance classes at The Dance Centre in London's Covent Garden.

"That was all two years ago now," she says, "since then I've been singing, playing and writing until we made the album last summer. Originally it was to be released last autumn but it kept getting delayed. I'm glad we waited until 1978 though. It kind of signifies it all starting with the new year for me."

And what a start.

The Kick Inside features thirteen of Kate Bush's own compositions. In addition to the aforementioned 'Wuthering Heights', there's 'The Man With The Child In His Eyes', a complex and intriguing song in which Bush probes the intricacies of a relationship between a young girl and an older man. 'Strange Phenomena', she explains, "is about how coincidences cluster together." On 'Kite' the versatile Bush assumes the pose of the inanimate flying machine to describe what might happen if a man could fly like a kite. 'Feel It', 'Oh To Be In Love' and 'L'Amour Looks Something Like You' deal insightfully with different angles of love, and 'James And The Cold Gun' tells about a man who leaves home to "live by the rifle" until the friends he left behind "get out of hand" and beg him to return.

The album was produced by Andrew Powell (whose credits include working with Alan Parsons and Cockney Rebel) and Dave Gilmour is listed as executive producer on 'The Man With The Child In His Eyes' and 'The Saxophone Song'. As a singer, Bush has an unusual and, once heard, addicting style. She possesses a breathtaking vocal range; her voice gracefully entwines with each individual note.

As a writer, she is amazingly insightful; blending the universal with the personal, she transcends both.

And, she has her own way of coaxing melodies from her beloved instrument.

"I feel as though I've built up a real relationship with the piano. It's almost like a person. If I haven't got a particular idea I just sit down and play chords and then the chords

almost dictate what the song should be about because they have their own moods."

The present has never been brighter for Kate Bush whose future looms as infinite as the uncharted stars.

"I'm really not sure how I'm going to develop from now," she explains, *"what direction my music will take. I just want to carry on exploring."*

EMI AMERICA

KATE BUSH, 'WUTHERING HEIGHTS' (prod. by A. Powell) (writer K. Bush (Glenwood, ASCAP) (3:33).

The record debuting in the US was number one for some time in Australia and the UK. Bush's voice is most unusual but continued listening and the lovely hook should endear it to pop and adult audiences alike. EMI America P-8003.

Kate was quoted in *Musician* in 1985; "I think probably most of the stuff I have liked, though, has actually been English, and possibly that's why my roots aren't American. Whereas perhaps with the majority of other people, well, you know, they were listening to Elvis and people like that and most of their heroes would have been American. But the artists I liked, such as Roxy Music and David Bowie, they were all singing in English accents and, in fact, were among the few in England who were actually doing so at that time. I mean to say, Elton John, Robert Palmer and Robert Plant sound American when they sing, although of course they're English... I was such a big fan of Elton John. I think really he was the first musical hero I had in that I aspired so much to what he was doing. I was just sort of starting to muck around writing songs, and then I saw this guy and he was the only one I'd ever seen who wrote songs and accompanied himself on the piano. And his playing was brilliant, and still today I think his playing is fantastic. It's always so right for his songs."

A lot of Kate Bush's appeal was in her eccentricity. It seems that overall, UK audiences understood and related to it enough for commercial success to come quickly. In the US however, they just didn't seem to get it. She did have a presence in the US though. It was in December 1978 that Eric Idle invited Kate to perform on NBC's *Saturday Night Live*. Regarding her appearance on the show, Kate said in an interview with MTV in 1985, "It was a lot of fun! It was really good. I was asked to come over here by Eric Idle from *Monty Python*, who was hosting the show. And it was a great honour for me and a real pleasure to do. Complete madness!"

On 20th May 1978, when Kate made an appearance on the British TV show *Revolver* (directed by Mickie Most), she was introduced by Peter Cook as "Basil Brush's younger sister, who had the great hit 'Withering Tights'." It hadn't taken very long at all for Kate to become so famous in the UK that her material could be joked about without the risk of the audience missing the reference.

***

Lionheart was recorded in 1978 between the months of July and September. It was released in November 1978, just nine months after *The Kick Inside*. *Lionheart* got to number six in the UK chart and it was certified platinum by the British Phonographic Industry. The second album was released so quickly after *The Kick Inside* so that EMI could capitalise on the success from her debut. It wasn't troublesome coming up with material for *Lionheart*; most of the songs on the album had been written even before *The Kick Inside* was made.

PETE
SILVERTON
FAILS TO
PENETRATE
WUTHERING
KATE'S
IMPREGNABLE
NICENESS

BUSH WHACKED

KATE BUSH as seen by the EMI publicity department (above) and by Janette Beckman (right).

AN HOUR or so in the company of Kate Bush is rather like being trapped for the duration as an unwitting participant in a very wholesome kids' TV show with definite but unwarranted intellectual aspirations. Blue Peter meets Tomorrow's World maybe. Pleasant, charming even, and certainly nice but ultimately insipid to the point of unreality.

Holding court in the two storey suite in Marble Arch's superficially distinguished Montcalm Hotel that EMI hired to present her to the day-long procession of journalist, she showed no signs of tiring by the time I arrived for the last session of the day's schedule. She was friendly, reservedly effusive in her greetings, smiled a lot and displayed an almost continual expression of wide-eyed innocence.

And, just as she was so nice, so were her answers to any questions I cared to offer up to her. I came out feeling that she'd talked for that hour or so very sweetly about absolutely nothing, that not once had she opened up even a tiny chink in her nice armour. Either she was an absolute professional determined not to reveal anything that would jibe with the image of sweet little Kate Bush that has been so casually but so carefully assembled since she was first unleashed on the nation's ears earlier this year . . . either that, or there really was nothing behind the facade and she really is that nice, that vacuous. (Or maybe you didn't ask the right questions. — Ed.)

Conversation is lightly sprinkled with five year old hip slang. She talks about 'vibes' refers to 'something I'm into' and frequently mentions her belief in 'coincidences'. She also continually explained her pet 'theories' — she seemed to have more of those than you'd find in a Ph.D. thesis on the nature of light. And, above all she was conscious of promoting the career of Kate Bush. Of course, that's true for virtually every interview — the talk which boosts the single which in turn launches the album — but she seemed more eager to grasp and exploit that route than most. Just about every move in her short public history was explained in terms of how it had served the purpose of promoting her artistic wares. Even the reason for this interview being done now and not in two months time, when her second album, 'Lion Heart' is released.

"I think mostly because the album's coming up and from now till the time the album is out this is the only time I'm going to have to do interviews and the reason why the timing's so tight is 'cos we've run over the time expected (recording the album). I think it's really just to let people know that the album's on its way . . .

"I don't really question it 'cos far as I'm concerned any publicity, any kind of communication that's getting from me to the public is good. I mean it can't be bad if people are hearing about you. Great. That's what it's all about — communicating to your public. And you can only do that directly on such a small level."

Although she insisted that she very much had complete control over her career at all points, I found it interesting that she'd shifted from her original position of saying she needed no manager to finding one, praising his abilities to the skies and then splitting from him and acquiring a new manager in Hilary Walker who sat upstairs and answered the phone throughout the interview.

"Well, that's something that I can't really talk about at the moment. It's something very personal between the two of us (her and her previous manager) that I can't really talk about now because if I do, er . . . um . . . it's gonna be very hard . . . were . . . er . . . um, y'know, we're in dealings at the moment that have to be sorted out and we're still friends and everything's fine. It was an agreement between the two of us and it's something that I'd like to talk to you about but if I do at the moment I could well get into trouble"

Forcefully rejecting any question of her taking her previous manager on court, she also talked about another aspect of her career which has had a similar on/off history — the promised live shows. First it was going to be sometime after the album was released, then more definitely this autumn and now Kate Bush on the road is promised for next year.

"Since the single ('Wuthering Heights') took off there was an awful lot of promotion needed in order to keep the momentum of it going in order to get the album through. And not only did it take off in this country but it took off in Holland . . . and other places. All my time is concentrated on getting myself established on some level or other around the world basically in as many countries as I could. The opportunity to do that is very rare for a new artist."

So the live dates were put off in favour of that kind of direct, business-decision type of promotion.

"Hopefully, we're heading for February to do England. It'll be pretty small places, medium sized theatres so I can get an intimate atmosphere which you don't get in those big gigs.

"I doubt if I'll take a large theatrical show. I do want to combine . . . what's the word? . . . theatre with music but I'm honestly not sure myself yet to what level I can take it. It's something very unexplored for me yet . . . I know what I'd like to do but whether I'm going to be able to do it I don't know because I haven't even started preparing for that yet. We're gonna start in October."

Probably like most people, I'd assumed she'd never done live gigs. In fact, she was the singer in the Kate Bush Band (what else!) for a while last year and she talked about that period as though it were part of a fondly remembered but long lost childhood, her affection for it for once obscuring the hesitance and inarticulacy of her speech.

"We did some pubs in the West End and around my area . . . south east London in the spring of '77. We just sort of did it for about five months . . . had a little band . . . it was great, very good experience. It was all other people's stuff . . . Stones, Beatles, Free. It was the first time I'd every sung anyone else's songs.

"It was at a time I'd just been staying home and writing songs a lot and going dancing (with Lindsay Kemp). And some friends of my brother turned up one day and I was on my way to get a train up to London to go dancing and I popped into see them and they were talking about forming a rock and roll band and they said they needed a singer and so I said 'Ooooo, yeah, great' and they said 'Right, first 'rehearsal two days time' and it was absolutely great, terrific".

Two of the members of that band are still with her and contributed to both 'The Kick Inside' and the new album. There was some indication earlier in the year that she was having to write to order for this second album.

"No, I could never feel that way about my songs. But it all happened fine. A month before I went in (to the studio) I was extremely worried about my material but it was okay because I had about three, four solid weeks in order to concentrate on that and I'd written about four, five new songs in that period. What I've done really is that there are quite a few old songs that I'd written about a year and a half ago that didn't go on the last album that I've rewritten which obviously isn't such a long process and they're exactly the way I would want them and they're on this album."

Predictably, she thinks the new album is better than 'Kick Inside' but, perhaps surprisingly she doesn't feel that she has changed much within herself.

"There is obviously a difference between me today and yesterday. I've got new skin molecules and everything. I'm probably a little more confident.

CONTINUES P. 23

74

KATE BUSH

FROM PAGE 21

sometimes not nearly as confident . . . I doubt the things I'm doing sometimes. I wonder if I really do believe in myself — I think they're very natural fears for someone to have."

But one thing she doesn't seem uncertain about is her sense of responsibility towards her audience.

"I did Ask Aspel the other week and there was one song that I really wanted to sing and I was really worried about singing largely to a child audience and it mentioned words like 'thighs' and I didn't want to sing that to children (sic) audiences. I was worried about the effect it would have on them and I sang a slightly milder song. I think of children and I don't want to sing about sex to them."

In that as in other ways she really does appear to be insufferably nice, the kind of picture of goodness that is boring because its origins seem so fundamentally passive.

"I've very, very, very rarely lost my temper. I've lost my temper once in the last year and that's the first time I've lost it in five or six years. I think losing your temper is a waste of time and a bloody nuisance. If you're uptight about something it's often your own fault so you should keep it to yourself. If someone does something that I'm really not into, if they're doing something to offend me or someone I love then I will assume annoyance to get at them but I don't really mean it.

"What's the point of losing your temper. It's an irrational, emotional reaction which does no good at all. It just makes people treat you like a hysterical . . . particularly in my position. If I was to jump up now, pull this table up, hit you on the head and take all my clothes off and jump out of the window . . . for the next year I would be called a tantrum maker."

Probably, once they'd given her a decent burial.

Somehow this emotional passivity seemed to fit in with her belief in psychic phenomena.

"It's like astrology. So many people say it's a lot of shit but real astrology, that's something that men spend years with real pure mathematics getting together."

No, she hadn't had her horoscope done — she's a Leo, whatever that signifies — but she had had her tarot cards read.

"They were quite amazing. I had them done in the November before the album came out and it practically predicted my success."

I suggested that maybe EMI should give up advertising and just cast the Tarot, Kate Bush smiled and the interview was over — she had to go straight into the studio.

She said goodbye cheerfully and I thanked her for the time. It was all very nice.

Of the ten songs on *Lionheart*, only 'Symphony In Blue', 'Fullhouse' and 'Coffee Homeground' were newly written for the album. However, all of the other songs that had been written long before Kate's rise to fame were reworked prior to the recording of the album. She was quoted in the *Liverpool Echo* in April 1979; "I take the majority of my ideas for songs from just watching and listening to people. It's people who make life, and that's where my songs come from... I have to work at it and it takes time, because I won't use a song until I'm really happy about it."

As with *The Kick Inside*, the songs on *Lionheart* were also inspired by a fascinating range of diverse ideas. In an interview with BBC Radio in 1979, Kate said, "'Kashka From Baghdad' actually came from a very strange American detective series that I caught a couple of years ago, and there was a musical theme that they kept putting in. And they had an old house, in this particular thing, and it was just a very moody, pretty awful serious thing. And it just inspired the idea of this old house somewhere in Canada or America with two people in it that no one knew anything about. And being a sort of small town, everybody wanted to know what everybody else was up to. And these particular people in this house had a very private thing happening."

Lionheart is the only one of Kate Bush's albums not to make it into the top five in the UK, but really, does that say something about the quality and relevance of the album? I would suggest that it perhaps doesn't — predominantly on the basis that commercial success isn't everything; getting to number six is still an impressive achievement and importantly, *Lionheart* was met with positive critical acclaim. Besides, it stayed in the chart well into 1979; its promotion was continued by 'Wow' as the second single and Kate's tour.

Lionheart spent a total of thirty-six weeks on the chart. The title of Kate's second album is from side one's closing track, 'Oh England My Lionheart'. In an interview with BBC Radio in 1979, she explained the idea behind the album's title; "I just think it's a great word, it sort of means hero, and I think hero is a very clichéd word, so I thought *Lionheart* would be a bit different." She said in a TV appearance on *Multi-Coloured Swap Shop* in 1979, "I guess I'm pretty fond of 'Oh England My Lionheart.'"

Kate was unhappy about the short period of time in which she was given to make *Lionheart*. She was quoted in *Pulse* in April 1984; "I was lucky to get it together so quickly but the songs seem to me, now, to be somewhat overproduced. I didn't put enough time into them."

She was quoted of the album in *Tracks* in November 1989; "It was rushed and that was responsible for me taking as much time as possible over albums. Considering how quickly we made it, it's a bloody good album but I'm not really happy with it."

Not only was it an issue of a lack of time, but a lack of space too. Kate was quoted in *Tune In* in December 1978; "Sometimes I get really worried because I'm not sure if I can ever write another song but that's often because I've not had enough time to get the flow going. It's very inspiring sometimes to write under pressure because you're in a very extreme emotional state and enjoying new experiences. What I do find a problem, is actually being left alone to put it on paper. I can't remember the last time I was alone for any length of time, even a day. It must be well over a year. I miss being by myself very, very much but it's very difficult because you can't just ask people to leave, they don't understand. When I was studying dance and writing songs I was alone a lot, but I was being so creative and I got so much done. I think it was probably one of the best times of my life — I was really happy."

Since *Lionheart*'s release, there have been multiple occasions where Kate has stated that she wasn't happy with the album. It really comes across that *Lionheart* was made under conditions that didn't favour Kate's preferred approach to making music. After all, it is one that she had established from a young age.

Paddy Bush was quoted in *Musician* in 1985; "To cultivate music you have to spend a lot of time by yourself, making a lot of very strange sounds over and over again. It's not the sort of thing you go hammering into others. When there's a family all in one house and you're getting your music together, normally the others in the family close the doors and try to keep the sound out. And when you've got several people playing instruments in the same house, well, things can get a bit complicated! I remember having things thrown at me during the early days because I was playing the same tune for six months. It would get people down! And when Kate began working on the piano, she'd go and lock herself away and wind-up spending five or six hours, seven days a week, just playing the piano... I mean, at the age of thirteen or fourteen she was spending tons and tons of time writing, but starting in fact when she was about ten." Kate was quoted in the *New Zealand Listener* in December 1978; "Sometimes I'd like a bit more time to myself. I'm really happy and I love to work, I think I need to and I feel good doing something really productive. I start feeling guilty if I'm wasting time."

At the time, perhaps there were doubts about how the public would respond to *Lionheart*. Kate was quoted of the album in *TV Week* in October 1978; "I can't explain what it's like… It's very hard to describe. Perhaps it's just a little bit more up-tempo than *The Kick Inside*."

The first single from *Lionheart* was 'Hammer Horror'. It just missed getting into the top forty in the UK with its highest position being number forty-four. John Peel wasn't a fan of the song. He said on BBC Radio in late 1978; "I'm not too enthused with this." Paul Gambaccini said of the single; "It gives me the impression of people dancing around a maypole on LSD. It doesn't grab me as immediately as 'The Man With The Child In His Eyes'."

'Hammer Horror' was reviewed in *Record Mirror* in November 1978; "Kate keeps up the formula and doesn't upset the fans… sounds like Joni Mitchell popping tabs with the London Symphony Orchestra. Offbeat, quirky and all that stuff."

It was reviewed in *Sounds* in the same month; "The non-thinking man's Joni Mitchell? Her approach is fresh and distinctive enough, but when you go a little deeper you find that unlike Joni Mitchell, there isn't much there."

It was reviewed in *New Musical Express*; "Chilling stuff — ominous post ELO orchestration with the unrequited lust of a broken affair viewed as living dead love bites back as in classic fifties British celluloid. A real nail biter, hypnotic and disconcerting. Catchy as all hell… What exactly are you on Kate Bush? And please can we have some?"

'Wow' was the next single to be released in the UK from *Lionheart*. Released on the back of her tour announcement, it became a top twenty hit; it peaked at number fourteen and also had success in other countries too. In some parts of the world, 'Symphony In Blue' was released as the second single from

Lionheart.

The cover of *Lionheart* showcases Kate sat in an attic wearing a lion costume. The photo was taken by Gered Mankowitz. The whole of *Lionheart* was recorded at Super Bear Studios in Berre-les-Alpes on the French Riviera. It is Kate's only album recorded outside of the UK. As with her debut album, her second was produced by Andrew Powell. In particular, Kate felt that she was still too inexperienced to produce an album herself (it wasn't until her third album, *Never For Ever*, that she took on the role of producer).

Lionheart was the first of Kate's albums to feature Del Palmer. He had previously played bass in the KT Bush Band. From *Lionheart* onwards, Palmer continued to contribute bass and his engineering skills on each of her albums up to and including the 2011 release, *50 Words For Snow*.

There are a range of references made to literature on *Lionheart*. 'In Search Of Peter Pan' makes references to J. M. Barrie's book. Literary references weren't necessarily something that Kate keenly aimed for; it comes across that it happened more organically than that. Upon being asked whether she planned to write more songs based on books, she was quoted in *Record Mirror* in February 1978; "Do you know, it's never occurred to me. I'd like to write another song connected to a book if the story was strong enough. It's not important though. I just want to carry on exploring. I like to write music about subjects I haven't touched before. That's my favourite thing."

The extent to which *The Kick Inside* hadn't garnered attention in the US was such that *Lionheart* went initially unreleased there. It wasn't until 1984, when Bush had more of a cult following from the release of *The Dreaming*, that *Lionheart* was released in the US.

Of course, as with *The Kick Inside*, *Lionheart* wasn't immune from getting a few bad reviews. The bad reviews picked up on similar things that 'Wuthering Heights' was criticised for. In November 1978, *New Musical Express* complained; ""Mature" lyrics sung in that twee irritating schoolgirl-siren voice… Actually most of the time she's nearer a vague British lineage — Barbara Dickson to Lynsey de Paul — than a Joni/Janis wonderland."

In the same month, *Record Mirror* stated; "A product which is at best moderate, lacking, and often severely irritating… The feel is often bland and soulless. Strictly MOR (middle of the road) with a clever tinge… This is flat conceived silliness… I simply dislike it and am not foolable."

It would certainly be drastically inaccurate to state that *Lionheart* was a flop though. It was reviewed in *Sounds* in November 1978; "I love her and I hate her, and you all feel exactly the same way only you're too unreal to confess the terrible crime… You have to take her seriously in spite of all the flying sneers and jeers… The songs themselves aren't individually strong at all. It's more the aura she creates… Winning and dreadfully insidious."

It was reviewed positively in the *Aberdeen Evening Express* in December 1978; "She has a voice which can be as delicate as a tinkling chandelier or as deep and powerful as a tolling bell. Yet it is constantly haunting. On this, her second album, Kate Bush displays her full vocal range on a set of ten numbers written by herself. The brooding new single, 'Hammer Horror', is the standout track and gives a good indication of the general atmosphere of this highly melodic album."

Lionheart wasn't unique in terms of the fact that it suffered a similar fate to what many second albums do; it was rushed to follow up on the success of a landmark debut album. Not only that, but it was released to a record buying public who held a combination of high expectations and cynicism in equal measure. With particular regards to Kate Bush and her public image at the time, some still thought she was just going to be a one hit wonder due to the eccentric qualities of 'Wuthering Heights'.

The overall feel of *Lionheart* isn't too dissimilar to that of *The Kick Inside*. This is the case in terms of the thematic explorations in Kate's lyrics as well as the arrangements and instrumentation; plenty of piano-led ideas, soaring vocals and effective use of a host of talented session musicians. Overall, it wasn't until the eighties that Kate's music began to take a different direction (she was quoted in the *Newcastle Journal* in January 1979; "With my new album, I feel ready to explore deeper, to make the sound heavier and with even more meaning for the listener.").

Kate was quoted in *Tune In* in December 1978; "Writing songs is what I'm good at and I really do feel it's what I'm meant to do. What I'm here for. I can't think of anything else that would be as fulfilling and I would be happy to be just a songwriter, full stop. But there are always new beginnings. As soon as you climb one wall, there's another wall to climb. The first album was a showcase, a foot in the door if you like, and it's very important for me to change and improve. I think I can be reasonably objective about my own work and I was lucky to get the songs together for *Lionheart*. There are no special themes because I always treat each song as a separate entity and work on them one at a time but I think many other songs are much more up-tempo. I love rock songs but normally they're just three chords and I don't believe in that sort of writing. I like a really strong melody line and that was a technique to learn but I seem to have cracked it. It's pleased me, anyway."

According to the *Melody Maker* end of year chart, Kate Bush emerged as the seventh in a list of the bestselling album artists of 1978 in the UK.

In January 1979, Kate began preparing for what would be her first live tour. The success of *The Kick Inside* is particularly noteworthy due to the fact that it wasn't promoted with a tour in 1978. *Superpop* reported in February 1979; "Up until the present time Kate has done virtually no live work apart from several carefully choreographed television appearances both here and abroad. With her latest album release, *Lionheart*, currently enjoying chart success, now seems the ideal time to tour. Although Bush has admitted apprehension at the prospect of playing to a captive audience she also regards it as an important part of being a true artist."

Kate was quoted in the same feature; "There's no pressure on me to tour, I've been told that the records will sell regardless. But I do feel that I owe people a chance to see me in the flesh (figuratively speaking). It's the only opportunity they have without media obstruction."

With 'Hammer Horror' not having done well commercially, by early 1979, it is understandable as to why some of the critics may have been suggesting the bubble had burst. However, behind the scenes, she was already working hard in preparation for her tour. It was entirely of her own direction in terms of concept, so much so that she didn't have a producer for the project.

At Covent Garden studio, Kate prepared rigorously for a tour consisting of an intricately choreographed show; over two hours of almost continuous singing and dancing. Having established the dance routines in terms of her role in the show, it was time to move the rehearsals to Shepperton Studios where everyone else involved in the show could be accommodated. Large mirrors were lined up opposite to the band in order that everyone could get an idea of how the whole thing was looking as it started to take shape.

During rehearsals, there were a number of practical things that needed to be worked out in terms of how best to arrange each track for the purpose of live performance. Upon being asked, "What will your backing band consist of when you go on tour?" in a TV interview on *Ask Aspel* in 1978, Kate replied,

"Well, we're not actually sure as yet because we're going to need quite a few extra musicians, because with the production on the album, people are going to expect to hear the same quality when they come to see us live. But we'll obviously have drums, probably two guitarists, bass, hopefully some kind of string quartet, if not a synthesiser player, keyboard player."

The chorography for each song required a lot of thought too. Kate said in a TV appearance on *Multi-Coloured Swap Shop* in 1979, "When you actually start working it out you find that you have very obvious limitations. You know, like you can't leap up into the air twenty times and keep singing a high A. You know, you'd soon explode into little pieces. But, I'm going to try to do something like that. I think theatre is a very important part of concerts."

In an interview with BBC Radio in 1979, Kate was asked, "Originally your Hippodrome date was supposed to be 4th March and it was put back a month, why was that?" She explained, "Well that was because of our rehearsal time, and in fact none of these dates should have got out. That was due to someone who was a bit naughty along the line. But we're coming out in April."

Although the tour was announced early in 1979, Kate and (nearly!) all others associated with it were secretive about what it would consist of, where and when. It was under conditions of complete confidentiality that the BBC had been filming preparations for the tour. Upon being asked what her live shows were going to be like, Kate joked in the BBC Radio interview; "Well I can't really tell you much about that because if I do you won't bother to come and see it… but I hope that you'll enjoy it, we're try to get something a bit special. But I really can't say much about it."

It wasn't until 3rd March that the details were announced in the UK music press. There is a sense that everyone was highly focussed on keeping their heads down and getting on with preparing for a show that needed to be as slick and as efficient as a well-oiled machine. By 15th March, ticket sales had been doing so well that it was necessary to add another two dates to the tour schedule. Two more performances were scheduled at the London Palladium and it wasn't long after that additional dates were also confirmed for Birmingham and Manchester too. The tickets sold at such a speed that the situation was taken advantage of by ticket touts.

'Wow' was released in March 1979. It was reviewed in *Record Mirror* that month; "An eerie gentle number with perceptive lyrics… the verses sound a little muddled but get better with playing."

It was reviewed in *Sounds* in the same month; "Apart from the body what does anyone see in this pantomime? I hear this mediocre chanteuse crooning her way through this silly song. I don't hear anything else at all… I realise that a lot of people would like to go to bed with her, but buying all her records seems a curious way of expressing such desires."

Still though, Kate won Best Female Artist in the British Rock And Pop Awards in April 1979. When she was nominated for three Ivor Novello Awards, she won with 'The Man With The Child In His Eyes' in the Best Lyric category.

The day after the Liverpool show that took place on 3rd April, *The Daily Mail* reported; "She exploded onto the stage a waif-like elfin figure in tight jeans and her voice pierced the auditorium with the bewitching quality of the wind shrieking over 'Wuthering Heights'… Kate relies not so much on the quality of her voice, but on the drama with which she sings her songs."

It was reported in the *Liverpool Echo* in April 1979; "What she gave the 2,500 fans — many of whom had queued all night when tickets went on sale a month ago — was much more than a concert: it was a show which combined ballet, theatre and rock into what the Americans are apt to call "a total experience." The simple fact is that Kate — virtually unknown twelve months ago, when she produced her first hit, 'Wuthering Heights' — does have real talent. Her music is real music, and not a collection of readily assembled chords. Her lyrics are intelligent, provocative, even poetic… She may only be 5ft 3in tall but she's a giant of a show woman. Then there's the personal charisma." To which Kate was quoted, "I'm probably the person who knows least about myself. To make music I need to be alone with my piano. I lock myself away."

A performance was reviewed in the *Birmingham Daily Post* in April 1979; "The Hippodrome was a highly appropriate venue for Kate Bush's Birmingham debut. It lent itself perfectly to the dramatic content of her show, which unfolded delightful effects. A specially designed set was complemented by the rapid costume changes, back projection slides, quick-fire lighting, darkness, ingenious props and some attractive illusionism in a generous show that stretched across three acts. Her highly personalised songs are well suited to such treatment. Like Genesis, her music follows a meandering path, washed through with a mix of subtle and exotic textures. The grandiose treatment that it embodied in the current show served to strengthen emotions that on vinyl are sometimes a trifle thin. It also served to reveal aspects of Kate Bush unbeknown to the record buying public. She is an accomplished dancer and freed from the handheld microphone she illustrated her emotions expressively, accompanied by two male dancers who complemented her movements. If the attractive setting was a bonus then we were not let down musically either. Kate Bush's voice is stunning, running the gamut from childlike high pitch through womanly maturity to a sexy rasp at the bottom, often twisting and turning its way rapidly over scattering phrases. And she gave every song in the Bush catalogue its due. Some such as the gorgeous 'The Man With The Child In His Eyes' were simple affairs backed only by her attractive piano playing.

Others, such as the storming 'Don't Push Your Foot On The Heartbreak' were full-blooded. And all to rapturous applause from the capacity house. In the meantime her eight piece band, which had the unenviable task of being both faultless and inconspicuous, achieved both admirably."

It was reported in the *Bristol Evening Post* in April 1979; "On last night's show she is a major artist by any standards. She wrote the songs, she sang them, and she danced beautifully with a sinuous grace… Each aspect was perfect in itself, together with imaginative staging, brilliant production, and a tight and disciplined backing group of musicians and dancers… It made for spectacular entertainment… A remarkable stage debut by a rare talent."

As well and music and dance, the show included poetry, mime and magicians. It played for twenty-eight dates across Europe. In a TV interview with VH-1 in 1990, Kate said, "We had a magician, and we had some poetry and just all different elements thrown together and it had a kind of a circus feel."

Not only was stamina needed for singing and dancing. Kate did costume changes between nearly every number. The innovative approach to the tour was such that the sound engineers developed a prototype for what became an early version of a microphone headset. It was made out of a wire coat hanger and used in the early shows. Kate was quoted in the *Liverpool Echo* in April 1979; "What matters most at the moment is being able to perform the songs I've written to the best of my ability, to give the public my everything, which is what they deserve."

In an interview with BBC Radio in 1979, Kate spoke of how much she valued keeping physically fit; "It's very important, because our bodies are what we live in. And we keep our homes clean, so we should keep our bodies clean. And I think exercise wakes you up. I mean, if I don't do any exercise my brain is asleep for most of the day. And if you just do a few sort of, you know — one, two, three… you feel much better, it's really wonderful… I'm vegetarian. But I'm not very good about what I eat, actually. I'm not that disciplined. I like chocolate and rubbish. But I love vegetables… I don't believe in eating life. I try to avoid eating life as much as I can. I mean there are things that I eat that probably have fat in them, and that. And, to a certain extent, I wear certain leather things. But I just don't believe in us considering ourselves so superior that we just go around killing everything and eating it… None of my family are really vegetarian. But it's just something I feel strongly about."

The tour was hard work, strenuous exercise was necessary in order to prepare physically and mentally. Kate was quoted in *Wireless* in September 1983; "It's something you can't just up and go out and do, you have got to build up for it. If I had tried to do it before all the training, I wouldn't have gotten through the first song. It's something you have to work into gradually. I don't know how I did it really. I think back now and I know I would pass out."

The tour had started off well but it was nearly cancelled when Kate was devastated by the fact that the lighting engineer, Bill Duffield, had fallen through an open panel in the lighting gallery of the stage at the warm up show at Poole Arts Centre and died the following week from his injuries. He was just twenty-one. Kate was shattered and contemplated cancelling the tour. "It was terrible for her", said band guitarist Brian Bath. "Kate knew everyone by name, right down to the cleaner, she was so like that, she'd speak to everyone. It's something you wouldn't forget, but we just carried through it."

Overall, the shows and the tours were a continued success but certainly, the behind the scenes tragic accident is undeniable. It was decided that a benefit show for a trust fund for Bill's family would take place on 12th May at Hammersmith Odeon.

Once the tour was over, Kate began work on her third

album with Jon Kelly. In September 1979, the *On Stage* EP was released. Featuring 'Them Heavy People', it got to number ten in the UK chart. Humble as ever, Kate had an invitation to appear in concert with the London Symphony Orchestra at the Royal Albert Hall as part of their 75th birthday celebrations on 18th November 1979. She was quoted in the *Daily Mirror* about it in October 1979; "It's a terrific honour but I thought about turning it down. I mean, it's a bit highbrow. But then I thought I'd look a bit stuck up if I did."

Kate wrote in the *Kate Bush Club* magazine in November 1979; "I hope it doesn't seem too strange having a special issue about the tour four months after it's finished. I think it's nice to have a chance to remember it all, especially as it's been uppermost in my mind recently, as I've been doing the mixing for the EP, which is out now. I've been in the studios a lot recently, recording new songs for the next album, and that has meant working with a lot of the band again, and I was really happy to work with Gary and Stewart (Gary Hurst and Stewart Avon-Arnold, two dancers who worked with Kate over the years) again when we did the video for *Top Of The Pops* (the video for the live EP version of 'Them Heavy People') I hope to be able to tell you about the songs I've been writing and recording soon. Take care."

The tour was perhaps a turning point for Kate Bush's rapport with those who had doubted her before as just as one hit wonder. It was considered in *The Daily Mail* in April 1979; "Kate Bush lines up all the old stereotypes, mows them down, and hammers them into their coffins with a show that is quite literally stunning. This quaint redhead turns pop upside down... how mediocre does she make most of her pop contemporaries seem."

In the second issue of the *Kate Bush Club* magazine in summer 1979, Kate wrote; "I must start by thanking you all for the masses of wonderful letters, and for all the slips that were left on the theatre seats that you took the time and trouble to send in. And the drawings, paintings, and poems have been great too. The tour was an incredible experience, and I'll never forget it, nor the reception we got from the audiences. In a way, the first night at Poole (this was the preview show held in Poole, the official premiere was given the following evening) was the most important, as it was the first real test as to whether it was going to happen or not, and the reaction really surprised me — it was lovely, and the greatest encouragement I could have possibly had. In fact, they all surprised me. I never expected such warmth. Some audiences wanted to be convinced, but that's only fair. In Europe people were a bit more reserved to start with in some places, especially where I wasn't well known, like France, but it was lovely — too good, really. I really hope people understand why I didn't talk to the audience during the show. It would have been out of place. On stage I'm not me, I'm trying to create a mood and character, and to speak is, I think, unnecessary. I was speaking in so many other ways that words were not really worth their money. I'd rather something complete and tight, than a few words that couldn't be heard clearly anyway because of the sound system. I was really thrilled that so many people have commented on the dancing, and I loved the things that were thrown on stage, especially the green frog that landed at my feet at such a perfect moment in 'Peter Pan', and a UFO t-shirt that I've been wearing a lot. It was a lovely surprise when people clapped when they recognised a song, especially the album tracks. Normally it's an honour to have the singles clapped, and it's great that people recognise the songs and know the music so well. All the audiences were very respectful, and that's the most one can expect. In the solo numbers I wondered if they were still there, they were so quiet."

She continued; "A lot of people have wondered why they couldn't use their cameras at the shows. I can understand why people want their own shots, but when the flash bulbs go off it's seen all over the auditorium and destroys the lighting effects on stage, spoiling it for everyone else. It's a bit selfish, like someone getting up to go out in the middle of a number, or shouting out. I'd like to be able to answer all your queries about live recordings and the video film, but at the moment not enough is known for me to say anything. But I'll let you know when something definite happens. What I really hated were the ticket touts. I wish something could be done to get rid of them, and I'm sure it could, as you don't see them on the continent. It's really sickening to hear of them selling forged tickets at obscene prices. Everyone was really upset by their disgusting presence everywhere we went. But that was the only negative thing about the tour. I was so sad when it was over, it was such a great time I never wanted it to end. Although it was right that it ended when it did, because we'd all paced our energies to that timing. I couldn't imagine a greater group of people to work with, and I think we all felt that it had been really worthwhile. Now I want to write some new songs and get together with my piano again — I feel I've neglected it for too long. I also want to learn how to cook pizzas, something I can't do at the moment, and want to be able to do."

At the end of 1979, Kate won *Melody Maker*'s Best Female Singer category for the second year running. At the same time, in the end of decade chart, *The Kick Inside* was announced as the UK's 71st bestselling album of the seventies — an impressive achievement considering that it was released towards the end of the decade. It was asserted in the *Reading Evening Post* in April 1979; "Many now consider her to be the most exciting arrival on the pop scene since Abba."

As dedicated as she was to her craft from the early days, even Kate herself was perhaps surprised at how it took off into being a career. She was quoted in *Pulse* in April 1984; "I didn't think I was going to do it for a profession. It was fun, something

I really enjoyed. I spent most of my time creating scenarios for songs. At sixteen I had gotten to the point where my songs were presentable. That was after five years of writing ballads and slow songs like 'The Man With The Child In His Eyes'." There's probably a lot to be said for the power of someone being motivated by the passion for what they're doing.

Kate recorded 'Wuthering Heights' with a new vocal track for inclusion on her 1986 compilation album, *The Whole Story*. Due to the popularity of the original recording, it is that which has been given the most airplay over the years. In an interview with BBC Radio in 1979, when asked whether she listened to her own records, Kate replied; "No, I don't actually. The only times I listen to them is when I've got a routine to work out. If I'm doing TV or something, then I have to listen through it to work out the routine. But that's the only time."

She was quoted in *Rolling Stone* in February 1994; "Albums are like diaries. You go through phases, technically and emotionally, and they reflect the state that you're in at the time."

As time moves on, it isn't uncommon for an artist to disengage somewhat with their earlier work. It is possible that Kate was no exception. Upon being asked, "Once an album finally exists, can you enjoy it or will you have nothing more to do with it?" she was quoted in *Musician* in 1985; "I couldn't with the first two albums as they didn't turn out the way I wanted them to, so obviously when I listened to them it was quite disappointing for me because I kept thinking of all the things I'd have liked to have done."

Kate was quoted regarding *The Kick Inside* in *Wireless* in September 1983; "That was such a long time ago. Some of those songs were written eight years ago. They feel a long way away and I haven't heard it in years, so I don't really know how I would react to it if I heard it. But the last time I heard it I was quite shocked by how young I sounded."

She was quoted of *Lionheart* in the same feature; "I thought that was very much a part of where I was with the first album and a lot of the songs were songs around the same time. I think in a way not much happened, it was really more of the same person."

In the *Kate Bush Club* magazine in 1984 a question was posed: "Do you compose your music with traditional written notation, or do you rely entirely on demo tapes? And has your process of composing melodies and harmonies, etc., changed since *The Kick Inside* and *Lionheart*? Are you, for example, more specific in writing out a bass line now than in 1978, or do you give more leeway to the other musicians during rehearsals than you used to?"

Kate responded, "My notation is very basic. I just write out the chords and lyrics, and I rely mainly on my memory. This does make it a bit difficult when I try to come back to a song after a few years, but I can listen to tapes and bash around on the piano, rediscovering the past. Before the first album it was easy: I used to practice all my songs every day in rotation and kept them totally in my head. But I just don't have the time any more so I do rely on the records and tapes to refer to chords — for live performances, for instance. I think the process of recording has changed very much since the first album, perhaps the biggest change being my involvement with the production. The demos on the first album were just piano and vocal; the demos for the second and third albums were a very big influence on the master recordings. The fourth album was completely influenced by the demos, and the current album is the demos. When working with musicians, I find that it depends totally on the individual, and the communication between the two of us. I will normally guide the direction to start with, but it's up to the musicians to make it really happen."

In an interview for Australian radio in 1985, Kate offered some context on how *The Kick Inside* related to her other albums up to that point; "I think it was probably the least experimental of all the albums. I'd written, say, two hundred songs from which we chose the thirteen songs that went on that. And it was recorded very quickly, there was very little time for experimentation. It was something that had a lot of forethought gone into it."

She was quoted of the album in *Tracks* in November 1989; "I'd wanted to make an album for such a long time so there was a great feeling of achievement. I hope I've matured since then. Some of those songs were written seven years before the album appeared."

In an interview with BBC Radio in 1982, Kate said of 'Wuthering Heights'; "It was the most successful single I've had, so that obviously does tend to stick in people's mind a lot. But as far as I'm concerned, I feel like I'm changing, hopefully with each album I do... It's especially my voice. I mean, in a way I'm still quite fond of some of the flavours of the old albums and some of the songs, but, my voice, it seems — it always sounds so young to me, because, you know, I feel that it's changing all the time."

Upon being asked, "How do you feel about your early records now?" Kate was quoted in *Kerrang!* in 1982; "I don't really like them. A lot of the stuff on the first two albums I wasn't at all happy with. I think I'm still fond of a lot of the songs, but I was unhappy about the way they came across on record." For context, this interview was done at the time when Kate was promoting her fourth album, *The Dreaming*.

Still though, there is no getting past the fact that *The Kick Inside*, and indeed 'Wuthering Heights', are what started it all. Kate said in a TV appearance on *Multi-Coloured Swap Shop* in 1979, "I think possibly I could get a problem with the fact that most people associate me with just one song. Then again I'm so lucky that people even remember me for anything, you know. I've been so lucky in this last year and really all I'm concerned about is just carrying on doing what I can and hoping that people will still like it."

In 1980, in a TV interview with *Profiles In Rock*, when asked, "Is there a special thing about the recording of the first album?" Kate replied, "Yes, I think there would be with anyone who was recording their first album, if they had been waiting for it for years, which I had. That was the one thing I wanted to do, it meant everything. To record an album was just like, God, you know, oh yeah!"

The success of Kate's debut was perhaps such that it put pressure on her writing process for later projects. In a TV interview on *Ask Aspel* in 1978, in response to the question of "Do you find it easier to write songs now, than when you were younger — is the process becoming easier?" Kate replied, "No, it's not easier. I find it's much more difficult, actually, because I'm much more critical of what I do. I mean, I used to just write loads of rubbish, and definitely lots of people think I still do, but it's a much more complicated process now, but I'm much more satisfied with the songs than I used to be. And I think that's good."

And then of course, there are the trappings of having to think commercially to maintain a sustainable career. Kate explained in the same interview; "I certainly have my idea of the singles that I want to release, and I put them forward. But they have to be agreed by the company, because obviously the company aims to sell records, and unless they think the single's capable, they're not going to release it. But so far we've agreed and it's been great."

Literary references remained a common theme in Kate's music. In an interview with MTV in 1985, Kate said, "'Cloudbusting' was inspired by a book that I found in a shop about nine years ago, it's out of print now. Written by a guy called Peter Reich, and it's called *A Book Of Dreams*. It's a very unusual, beautiful book, written by this man through the eyes of himself when he was a child, looking at his father, and the relationship between them. A very special relationship, his father meant so much to him. His father was a psychoanalyst, very respected, but he also had a machine that could make it rain, and the two of them would go out together and they would make it rain. And in the book there was such a sense of magic, that it a way the rain was almost a presence of his father. Unfortunately, it's a very sad book in that the peak of it is where his father was arrested, taken away from him, because of his beliefs he's considered a threat. And it's how the child has to cope from that point onwards without his father. And the song is really using the rain as something that reminds the son of his father. Every time it rains, instead of it being very sad and lonely, it's a very happy moment for him, it's like his father is with him again."

From the nineties onwards, Kate Bush's musical output and public appearances decreased, earning her a reputation for being an enigmatic recluse. I would suggest that the logic behind such reputation is perhaps a little flawed as in, does an artist always have to be in the limelight to be regarded as something other than a recluse? Perhaps that's the nature of the fame game as some people might choose to see it. Besides, no matter how you look at it, in the length of her career to date, Kate has worked with Peter Gabriel, Prince and Elton John. She has also been a tremendous source of inspiration for other artists such as Björk and Tori Amos.

Being famous perhaps comes with a fair amount of pressure. Kate said in an interview with BBC Radio in 1979; "In fact, now I feel a lot more worried about how I look than I ever have done, because of all this emphasis on the way I look. Because I'm performing I do have a very different way of looking when I'm quite normal."

She was quoted in the *Daily Mirror* in October 1979; "I thought I was a bit of a freak and got really paranoid, you know, people wanting to stare all the time and touch you. Since the tour finished I've been okay, but I still feel self conscious when I sign autographs… I'm a loner, really. I don't have an extravagant love life or go to wild parties."

She was quoted in the *Daily Mirror* in August 1979; "Being a pop singer isn't always fun. It isn't all parties and the glamorous life. I miss being able to have a close relationship." In 1980, in a TV interview with *Profiles In Rock*, Kate mused, "I don't think I enjoy being famous. You see famous is one of those words, isn't it, it's so created. Sometimes, it's a buzz, being honest, sometimes it really is a buzz. But a lot of the time it embarrasses me, it makes me feel awkward with the people I'm with, because they get embarrassed. But it's something I'm learning to accept. They're just saying hello in their own way."

There certainly wasn't another tour on the cards for the foreseeable future. In an interview with MTV in 1985, Kate said, "I'd really like to tour again and the one tour I did in '79, England and Europe, was really exhausting. We rehearsed it for maybe six months and by the time we got around to the first night, I was really looking forward to having an audience out there so that you could how you see how they would react, see if they liked it. It was really a lot of fun and in many ways very educational for me as a performer as well as a person. But it's the commitment, it's so much time and effort. And I just don't know if it's something I want to launch into. It'd probably be a year out, at least."

Kate was quoted of her 1979 tour in *Rolling Stone* in February 1994; "I did enjoy it, but I was really physically exhausted. Eventually, I got nervous about performing live again, because I hadn't done it for so long, and I think I actually started losing a lot of confidence as a performer. I felt that I'd become a writer in a very isolated situation, just working with a small group of people. The more I got into presenting things to the world, the further it was taking me away from what I was, which was someone who just used to sit quietly at a piano and sing and play. It became very important to me not to lose sight of that. I didn't want my feet to come off the ground... Touring is an incredibly isolated situation. I don't know how people tour for years on end. You find a lot of people who can't stop touring, and it's because they don't know how to come back into life. It's sort of unreal... It's very moving that a lot of people that I don't know are so supportive of what I do. I don't tour, I don't give them that much, really. Obviously I try to make the best music that I can, but after about two years of making an album you start to worry: 'Is it going to come out all right? Is it all going to sound churned out?' And then you get odd little letters from fans here and there encouraging you, and that's a fantastic boost. I suppose I hope that if I keep an integrity in my work, then they'll always feel that."

Even at the height of her fame, Kate seemed keen to challenge the media. Perhaps it's one of those things that can be a pain to deal with. In response to the question of "Is it true that you're going to make a film called *The Gold Plated Dream Machine* with the motorcycle stunt rider Eddie Kidd?" she wrote in the *Kate Bush Club* magazine in November 1979; "No, it isn't, and I've never even heard of it. You mustn't believe everything (or anything?) you read in the papers. Quite a lot of articles irritate me because of their inaccuracy. It would be so easy for a journalist to send me the copy of what they've written so I could check up on the facts — not of their opinion, which is their own business — but on the facts; and so far, not one has done so. Nearly every interview is distorted in some way. That's one of the reasons for starting this club, so that I can give you the genuine facts that you want to know." (In an interview with MTV in 1985, Kate said, "Never at any point in my life have I wanted to be an actress. But if there was something offered that was interesting enough, I would certainly want to do it, yes.")

Interestingly, over the last few decades, a lot has been written about Kate Bush from a feminist perspective. Whether or not Kate herself approached her work from such angle is very much open to interpretation. In an interview with BBC Radio in 1979, she said, "I'm always getting accused of being a feminist. Really I do write a lot of my songs for men, actually. In fact, 'In The Warm Room' is written for men because there are so many songs for women about wonderful men that come up and chat you up when you're in the disco and I thought it would be nice to write a song for men about this amazing female. And I think that I am probably female-oriented with my songs because I'm a female and have very female emotions but I do try to aim a lot of the psychology, if you like, at men."

The link with feminism is perhaps understandable though in view of how Kate wrote about women in her songs. She was quoted in *Record Mirror* in February 1978; "When I first read *Wuthering Heights* I thought the story was so strong. This young girl in an era when the female role was so inferior, and she was coming out with this passionate, heavy stuff. Great subject matter for a song. I loved writing it. It was a real challenge to précis the whole mood of a book into such a short piece of prose. Also, when I was a child I was always called Cathy, not Kate, and I just found myself able to relate to her as a character. It's so important to put yourself in the role of the person in a song. There's no half measures. When I sing that song I am Cathy."

Kate was quoted in *Record Mirror* in February 1978; "I want it (success) to stand on the weight of my work, not what I look like. I realise people are going to capitalise on it. It annoys me though. Why should people want to know about my sex life? It's completely irrelevant to what I'm doing. I give them everything they need to know about me in my songs, because they are personal songs. Being regarded as a sex object just gets in the way most of the time unless it's relevant to the role

I'm playing in the song. Guys get it, of course, but only those that seem to ask for it. Girls seem to get it whether they want to be regarded in that way or not. To overplay it is wrong. It can't possibly last."

Some might even say that Kate did something pioneering for female artists. She was quoted in *Kerrang!* in 1982; "Now it's much easier for females to be recognised (as singer/ songwriters) because there are more around, but when I started there was really only me and Debbie Harry, and we got tied into the whole body thing. It was very flattering, but not the ideal image I would have chosen... I've spent so much time trying to prove to those people that there's more to me than that. Just the fact that I'm still around and my art keeps happening should convince them I can't go around all the time telling people where I'm at now. I just have to hope that there are people who see the changes and change with me. I think it was just that the media didn't know how to handle it, because it was so unusual at the time... I felt that because I was so young people weren't taking me seriously. They couldn't accept that I could be so involved in what I was doing."

Overall, *The Kick Inside* is a very balanced album instrumentally. The piano is pretty much omnipresent but it doesn't overpower the guitars, bass or drums. Everything works well together to contribute towards songs that are generously textured. It makes for a listening experience that offers a lot of interest in terms of replay value. Love her or loathe her, Kate Bush stormed the UK charts in 1978 in a way that was attention grabbing, and deservedly so.

Artistically, her work was one of a kind and it is still an iconic talking point to this very day. Whether her work is viewed through a lens of what it is to be a young woman in the public eye or simply, as the output of a musician in their own right at the beginning of their career, the fact remains that *The Kick Inside* is full of wonder and intrigue. With regards to music innovation and music history, it matters.

The Kick Inside -
A Comprehensive Discography

Album Personnel

Musicians
Kate Bush - piano, lead vocals, backing vocals
Andrew Powell - arrangements, keyboards (2), piano, Fender Rhodes (3), bass guitar, celeste (6), synthesiser (9), beer bottles (12)
Duncan Mackay - piano, Fender Rhodes (1, 10), synthesiser (3), Hammond organ (4, 6, 7), clavinet (4)
Ian Bairnson - electric guitar, acoustic guitar (except on 2), backing vocals (9), beer bottles (12)
David Paton - bass guitar (1, 3, 4, 7, 9–12), acoustic guitar (6, 9), background vocals (9)
Stuart Elliott - drums (exc. 2, 5, 13), percussion (9, 12)
Alan Skidmore - tenor saxophone (2)
Paul Keogh - electric guitar, acoustic guitar (2)
Alan Parker - acoustic guitar (2)
Bruce Lynch - bass guitar (2)
Barry de Souza - drums (2)
Morris Pert - percussion (3, 4, 6), boobam (12)
Paddy Bush - mandolin (9), backing vocals (11)
David Katz - orchestral contractor (for an unnamed orchestra on all tracks except 4, 5, 7, 8, 12)

Production
Andrew Powell - producer
David Gilmour - executive producer (2, 5)
Jon Kelly - recording engineer
Jon Walls - assistant engineer
Wally Traugott - mastering

Track Listing

Side one
1. Moving (3:01)
2. The Saxophone Song (3:51)
3. Strange Phenomena (2:57)
4. Kite (2:56)
5. The Man With The Child In His Eyes (2:39)
6. Wuthering Heights (4:28)

Side two
7. James And The Cold Gun (3:34)
8. Feel It (3:02)
9. Oh To Be In Love (3:18)
10. L'Amour Looks Something Like You (2:27)
11. Them Heavy People (3:04)
12. Room For The Life (4:03)
13. The Kick Inside (3:30)

Country by Country

Releases for the main territories are listed, along with unusual versions from around the world.

UK:
EMI, EMC 3223, 17th February 1978, LP
EMI, TC-EMC 3223, 17th February 1978, cassette

Reissues:
EMI, CDP 7 46012 2, 1979, LP (Picture disc)
EMI, CDP 7 46012 2, 1984, CD
Fame, FA 3207, September 1988, LP
EMI, LPCENT 5, 1997, LP

Parlophone, 0777 7 46012 2 1, 2015, CD
There have been multiple reissues of both the LP and CD with variations such as label designs etc. using the original catalogue numbers for each.

US:
Harvest, SW-11761, March 1978, LP
It's unclear if this first release was also issued on cassette or 8-track cartridge.

Reissues:
Capitol Records, 4XW-11761, 1978, cassette
Capitol Records, 8XW-17003, 1978, 8-track cartridge*
*To accommodate the format the tracks were arranged as follows:

Program 1
1-1	Moving
1-2	The Saxophone Song
1-3	Room For The Life

Program 2
2-1	Strange Phenomena
2-2	Kite
2-3	The Man With A Child In His Eyes
2-4	L'Amour Looks Something Like You

Program 3
3-1	Wuthering Heights
3-2	Feel It
3-3	Them Heavy People

Program 4
4-1	James And The Cold Gun
4-2	Oh To Be In Love
4-3	The Kick Inside

All of the above US versions have a different cover to the UK version. It is of Kate clutching her hair; also used in Canada.

EMI America, SW-17003, July 1978, LP
EMI-Manhattan Records, E1-46012, 1987, LP
EMI-Manhattan Records, CDP 7-46012-2, 1987, CD
All of the above versions have an entirely different sleeve from the other US releases and have a photo of Kate in a wooden box.

Japan:
EMI, EMS-81042, 20th May 1978, LP
EMI, ZR25-195, 20th May 1978, cassette

Reissues:
EMI, CP35-3045, CD, 1983, CD
EMI, EMS-63026, 1984, LP
EMI-Manhattan Records, CDP 7-46012-2, 1987, CD*
*US pressing for Japanese market with obi strip and second US cover design.

EMI, CP21-6082, 8th November 1989, CD
EMI, TOCP-3005, 31st May 1995, CD
EMI, TOCP-67815, 2nd November 2005, CD
EMI, TOCP-67815, 26th September 2008, CD
EMI, TOCP-54212, 26th October 2011, CD
EMI, TOCP-54212, 5th June 2013, CD
Parlophone, WPCR-80047, 29th January 2014, CD

All Japanese releases have a unique cover design with a photo of Kate in a pink top, with the exception of the US pressing done for the Japanese market. Those listed with the same catalogue number were reissued with different obi strips.

Germany:
EMI, 1C 064-06 603, 1978, LP
EMI, 1C 264-06 603, 1978, cassette

Reissues:
EMI, CDP 7 46012 2, 1984, CD
Parlophone, 0777 7 46012 2 1, 2015, CD
There have been multiple reissues of both the LP and CD with variations such as label designs etc. using the original catalogue numbers for each.

Other releases of interest:
Jugoton, LSEMI 70870, Yugoslavia
Unique cover with photo of Kate in a white dress.

EMI, SLPE 500.750, Uruguay
Unique cover with monochrome face photo of Kate.

EMI, CMC 1049, Sweden, cassette
1988 reissue with unique cover. Full height shot of Kate
dancing in a white dress. Not known if it was released in other
formats.

Singles
Four single couplings were released from the album.

Wuthering Heights / Kite
EMI, EMI 2719, 20th January 1978, UK
This coupling was also released in the following territories:
EMI America, 8003, US
Harvest, 4589, Canada
EMI, 1C 006-06 596, Germany
Sonopresse, 2S 006-06596, France
EMI, 3C 006-06596, Italy
EMI, 4C 006-06596, Belgium
EMI, 5C 006-06596, Netherlands
EMI, 7C 006-06596, Sweden
EMI, 10 C 006-006596, Spain
Tonpress, S-120, Poland
EMI, 31C 006 06596, Brazil
EMIJ 4206, South Africa
EMI-11678, Australia
EMI 2719, New Zealand
EMI, EMI 2719, Argentina
EMI, EMI 500 045, Uruguay

EMI, EMI 8148, Mexico
EMI, EMI 103-0140, Ecuador

Moving / Wuthering Heights
EMI, EMR-20417, 6th February 1978, Japan
Other sources say this was released 20th April.

The Man With The Child In His Eyes / Moving
EMI, EMI 2806, 12th May 1978, UK
This coupling was also released in the following territories:

EMI America, 8006, US
Harvest, 72798, Canada
EMI, 1 C 006-06 712, Germany
Sonopresse, 2S008.06712, France
EMI, 4 C 006-06 712, Belgium
EMI, 5C 006-06712, Netherlands
EMI, 8E 006 06712, Portugal
Tonpress, S-171, Poland
EMI, EMIJ 4220, South Africa
EMI, EMI-11743, Australia
EMI, EMI 2806, New Zealand
'The Man With The Child In His Eyes' has an added spoken/acapella intro, not on the album.

Them Heavy People / The Man With The Child In His Eyes
EMI, EMR-20490, 5th September 1978, Japan

Also 'Strange Phenomena' was released as a single in Brazil coupled with 'Wow' from *Lionheart* on 1st June 1979: EMI, EMI 31C 006 07070.

1979 Tour

April

Monday 2nd	Arts Centre, Poole, England (warm up concert)
Tuesday 3rd	Empire Theatre, Liverpool, England (opening night)
Wednesday 4th	Hippodrome, Birmingham, England
Thursday 5th	Hippodrome, Birmingham, England
Friday 6th	New Theatre, Oxford, England
Saturday 7th Southampton,	Gaumont Theatre, England
Monday 9th	Hippodrome Bristol, England
Tuesday 10th	Apollo, Manchester, England
Wednesday 11th	Apollo, Manchester, England
Thursday 12th	Empire Theatre, Sunderland, England
Friday 13th	Usher Hall, Edinburgh, Scotland
Monday 16th	Palladium, London, England
Tuesday 17th	Palladium, London, England
Wednesday 18th	Palladium, London, England
Thursday 19th	Palladium, London, England
Friday 20th	Palladium, London, England
Tuesday 24th	Konserthuset, Stockholm, Sweden
Thursday 26th	Falkoner Theatre, Copenhagen, Denmark
Saturday 28th	Congress Centre, Hamburg, Germany
Sunday 29th	Carré Theatre, Amsterdam, Netherlands

May

Wednesday 2nd	Kongresszentrum Liederhalle, Stuttgart, Germany
Thursday 3rd	Circus Krone, Munich Germany
Friday 4th	Gürzenich, Cologne, Germany
Sunday 6th	Théâtre des Champs-Élysées, Paris, France
Tuesday 8th	Mannheimer Rosengarten, Mannheim, Germany
Thursday 10th	Jahrhunderthalle, Frankfurt, Germany
Friday 12th	Hammersmith Odeon, London, England (benefit concert for Bill Duffield's family)
Saturday 13th	Hammersmith Odeon, London, England
Sunday 14th	Hammersmith Odeon, London, England

Set List

Moving
The Saxophone Song
Room For The Life
Them Heavy People
The Man With The Child In His Eyes
Egypt
L'Amour Looks Something Like You
Violin
The Kick Inside
Interlude — John Carder Bush poetry reading
In The Warm Room
Fullhouse (not performed at the Hammersmith Odeon dates in London)
Strange Phenomena

Hammer Horror (not performed live)
Kashka From Baghdad
Interlude — Chanting
Don't Push Your Foot On The Heartbrake
Wow
Coffee Homeground (with extended instrumental introduction)
In Search Of Peter Pan
Interlude — John Carder Bush poetry reading
Symphony In Blue (contains elements of Gymnopédie 1 by Erik Satie)
Feel It (with instrumental introduction)
Kite
James And The Cold Gun
First encore
Oh England My Lionheart
Second encore
Wuthering Heights

All the tracks from *The Kick Inside* as well as *Lionheart* were performed as part of the concerts, along with two tracks 'Egypt' and 'Violin' that appeared on the third album *Never For Ever* in 1980.
On 24th, 26th, 28th and 29th April, 'In the Warm Room', 'Kite', 'Oh England My Lionheart', and 'Wuthering Heights' were dropped from the set because Kate was suffering from a throat infection.
'Fullhouse' was not performed on 13th and 14th May.
The 12th May benefit concert 'In Aid Of Bill Duffield' featuring guest stars Steve Harley and Peter Gabriel had a different setlist as follows:

Moving
Symphony In Blue
Violin
The Kick Inside
Strange Phenomena
Hammer Horror
Kashka From Baghdad
Don't Push Your Foot On The Heartbrake
Them Heavy People (with Peter Gabriel & Steve Harley)
The Woman With The Child In Her Eyes (with Peter Gabriel
& Steve Harley)
The Man With The Child In His Eyes
Here Comes The Flood (Peter Gabriel)
I Don't Remember (Kate Bush & Peter Gabriel)
D.I.Y. (Peter Gabriel)
Best Years Of Our Lives (Steve Harley)
Come Up And See Me (Make Me Smile) (Steve Harley)
Wow
Kite
James And The Cold Gun
Wuthering Heights
Let It Be (with Peter Gabriel & Steve Harley)

Personnel
(from the Kate Bush tour programme available at the concerts)

Performers
Ben Barson - synthesiser, acoustic guitar
Brian Bath - electric guitar, acoustic mandolin, background

vocals
Kate Bush - vocals, piano, keyboards
Paddy Bush - mandolin, background vocals, various
instruments

Simon Drake - magician
Glenys Groves - background vocals
Preston Heyman - drums/percussion
Kevin McAlea - piano, keyboards, saxophone, 12-string guitar
Alan Murphy - electric guitar, whistles
Del Palmer - bass guitar
Liz Pearson - background vocals

Production
Conception, producer, director - Kate Bush
Production design, stage direction - Dave Jackson
Stage management - Nick Levitt
Stage crew - Cliff Carter, Martin Prior, Gerry Raymond
Barker, Andrew Bryant
Costuming - Lisa Hayes
Costuming assistance - Hermione Brakspear
Choreography - Anthony Van Laast

Audiovisuals
Sound engineering - Gordon Patterson
Projections - Ken Sutherland
Lighting consulting - James Dann
Spoken word and poetry - John Carder Bush
Photography - Gered Mankowitz, Terry Walker, Hirchono

Tour management
Promotion - Lindsay Brown
Tour management - Richard Ames
Programmes - Kate Bush, Nicholas Wade, Nick Price
Tour graphics and merchandise - Paul Maxwell Ltd.
Tour co-ordination - Hilary Walker, John Carder Bush

In-depth Series

The In-depth series was launched in March 2021 with four titles. Each book takes an in-depth look at an album; the history behind it; the story about its creation; the songs, as well as detailed discographies listing release variations around the world. The series will tackle albums that are considered to be classics amongst the fan bases, as well as some albums deemed to be "difficult" or controversial; shining new light on them, following reappraisal by the authors.

The first four titles published were:
Jethro Tull - Thick As A Brick	*978-1-912782-57-4*
Tears For Fears - The Hurting	*978-1-912782-58-1*
Kate Bush - The Kick Inside	*978-1-912782-59-8*
Deep Purple - Stormbringer	*978-1-912782-60-4*

Other titles in the series:
Deep Purple - Slaves And Masters
Emerson Lake & Palmer - Pictures At An Exhibition
Korn - Follow The Leader
Jethro Tull - Minstrel In The Gallery
Kate Bush - The Dreaming
Elvis Costello - This Year's Model
Deep Purple - Fireball
Talking Heads - Remain In Light
Jethro Tull - Heavy Horses
Rainbow Straight Between - The Eyes
The Stranglers - La Folie

CPSIA information can be obtained
at www.ICGtesting.com
Printed in the USA
BVHW050255100621
609093BV00008B/1040